OMG! You're Not Married ... Yet?

All websites listed herein are accurate at the time of publication, but may change in the future or cease to exist. The listing of website references and resources does not imply the author's endorsement of the site's entire contents.

All Scripture references have been arrived at through the use of the website BibleGateway.com. Those marked KJV are taken from the King James Version, NIV – New International Version, NKJV – New King James Version.

Edited by: Yonique Lawrence & Douladel Patrice Willie
Author Photo: Shavado Bastian

ISBN : 978-976-8230-50-8

This book is dedicated to

My father, whose advice in the summer of 1997 could have not been more poorly timed in my eyes, but undoubtedly followed God's perfect timing. It has forever etched in my mind the need to make even the seemingly most insignificant date one of which God would approve.

Pastor Gary Williams whose counsel and work in youth ministry have impacted me more than he could ever know.

CONTENTS

Note to the Reader

I had to do this

"I'm not saying I have this all together, that I have it made. But I'm well on my way, reaching out for Christ, who has so wonderfully reached out for me. "

Philippians 3:12 (The Message)

From my observations, I am persuaded that there are basically three types of married people: firstly, those who got married because they thought it was the next appropriate step for their stage in life; secondly, those who saw marriage as an avenue of escape from a difficult situation - perhaps an unplanned pregnancy, severe struggles in maintaining sexual purity in a committed relationship, or a business/social/immigration necessity; and thirdly, those who believed that this spouse would complement them in personality and life goals. Fortunately or unfortunately, depending on your take on the necessity of a life-long partner, I do not fit into any of those groups and as such cannot be married as yet. The idea for this book was birthed from a feeling that I had to "defend" why, post twenty-five years, I was still single. Additionally, I felt compelled to highlight some of the struggles I have faced in my own life and have observed in the lives of others who are unmarried; and outline necessary *Biblical* steps to surmount these obstacles.

Though appropriate for anyone to read, this book is targeted primarily at single Christian individuals who have perhaps struggled with the negative attitude often given to single adults, those who may see marriage only as an avenue of legitimizing their sexual urges, as well as those who believe that marriage will somehow fill inadequacies they have in their own lives. I am being extremely cautious with my tone lest I give the impression that I am anti marriage. Quite the contrary, I believe marriage can be a beautiful experience but refuse to be married only as an alternative to remaining single. My pastor, Wilbur Outten of Freeport Bible Church, Bahamas, often refers to himself as that beggar who has found bread and as such is showing others how to do the same; and this is my intention with this book. Like the lepers of 1 Kings 7, I am opening myself to scrutiny even ridicule because I want to let the starving single know that their hunger will not be satisfied by a mere diet of marriage. Instead, satisfaction is just beyond the city walls if they are willing to step outside of that paradigm society has created around them, one that makes them believe their lives are incomplete if they are single. Singleness is a natural aspect of life and it does not necessarily speak to a flaw in an individual's character. Like me, many persons have to learn to accept, that nothing is wrong with them.

It was Toni Morrison who said *"If there's a book you really want to read and it hasn't been written then you must write it"*. Strangely, few resources are available on the issue of living singly as a committed, born again believer in Jesus Christ, though singleness is a stage in all our lives. Not surprising is the fact that it is a life many do not understand how to live. This therefore is my story; my story of a discovery of happiness, a discovery of an enriched, purpose-filled, single life. With the Holy Spirit and the Scriptures as my guide I seek to shed some light on some of the misgivings of a single person's life, as well as highlight the path I took to liberate myself from the view that I was somehow on *pause* till I 'found a Mr. Right'. For several years, I believed that in order to validate who I was as a woman I would have to sport a diamond (or some other wedding band type jewel) on the third finger of my left hand. I have learned however *"... in whatever state I am, to be content."*[1] This contentment, I might add is not superficial. I am not trying to make myself believe I am happy. I genuinely am. This happiness stems from a realization of who I am and why I am. It does not translate to a perfect life, but living in awareness that my entire life is in God's complete control and *"... no plan [of the Lord's] can be thwarted"*.[2] Should God lead me to a marriage however, I will look at it as another phase of the life that I must live to complete God's big picture.

Daniele

[1] Philippians 4: 11 NKJV
[2] Job 42:2 NIV

ACKNOWLEDGMENTS

My final year in college was a rough one; and the parting words from my research paper supervisor were *"Be sure not to become a teacher because you can't write."* Of course I knew her bitter admonition had very little to do with my penmanship and everything to do with what she thought of my stylistic abilities. Those words burned me thoroughly and have sometimes caused waves of doubt to sweep over me during my ten year teaching career. Back then I vowed that in the first book I would write, I would name her in a sarcastic dedication as a declaration that she was wrong. Maturity has taught me however to use even seemingly negative criticism by finding whether it has some merit lying beneath. Whether a successful career in writing will be achieved is up to God; but it is undeniable that eleven years later, I am a far better writer than when I sat under her tutelage. Her criticism has over the years fueled my passion to work hard and this is why I refer to her in this section of the book, for in some odd way, she deserves a measure of credit for the work that I have done; as her vote of *no confidence* has given me drive.

It would be remiss of me not to thank those who have given feedback and have helped in other ways to guide the direction of this book in order to ensure that it is both relevant and scripturally sound.

Most importantly, I thank my Lord and Savior, Jesus Christ, for the two most treasured possessions in my life: my relationship with him that has over the years been tested and stretched but has had immeasurable success because of his unmoving hand; and the supportiveness of a family that brings tears of joy to my eyes when I think about them. To my father, Derek, my mother, Joan and my sister, Douladel Patrice: suitable words that express the degree of gratitude and love that I have for you escape me. The world would be so much more loving and peaceful if more people understood what it meant to love as unconditionally as you have – disagreeing and reprimanding, yet still never severing those cords of love that, through Christ, hold us together. During my childhood our house had a wall plaque that read *"The family that prays together stays together"*. Every morning during my years in high school, later over the telephone during my college years and now across the miles the message of that plaque continues to govern our family. I thank God for that, and I thank God for you.

INTRODUCTION

As I compiled information for this book I formulated my top ten reasons NOT to marry. Incidentally these often form the bases for why some people actually decide to *take the plunge*. I can almost attach the names of persons I know beside some of these reasons. Fortunately for many of them, they have matured and their development has helped their marriages to blossom. There have been a few however who have not been as fortunate and they have separated or have been unfaithful to their spouses, they live in bitter marriages and 'endure' for the sake of their children or appearances, others are in the process of, or have already divorced. Here, in descending order, are my ten primary reasons a couple should **NOT** do nuptials.

10 Church/ Social pressure

9 It's time (I'm ___ years old)

8 Financial deliverance

7 We've been dating *forever*

6 To fill a void

5 Desire for children

4 Attractiveness (looks)

3 My child/children need a mother/father

2 Guilt (I'm pregnant/ she's pregnant)

1 Legitimize sexual activity

These reasons are subjective and have been arrived at through personal interpretation of what I have observed of those around me. Since there are reasons individuals should not get married, I believe there will be reasons an individual should get married. The number one reason any person, especially a believer, should get married is: ***God has revealed it in your spirit that you can serve His purposes just as well or better by being joined with a similarly focused individual.*** Sounds super spiritual? How many people, believers included, even bring God into the center of their decision to be married? The Divorce Courts are filled with petitions of persons who joined because of one or more of the reasons I mentioned above. If you and I are truly honest with ourselves, we have desired or even married persons for those very reasons.

Interestingly however, those things we often think of as being most important, such as the ones included in my earlier list are in reality supplementary. One of God's earliest commands to mankind was that we be fruitful and fill the earth[3]. Therefore, once they are physically able, having children is a natural result of a union between a man and a woman. I would however dare anyone to suggest that it should be *the* reason behind that union. Many

[3] Genesis 1:28

too have walked the aisle in a bid to 'fix' an illicit sexual relationship: he has *made an honest woman out of her* and she has convinced him to *buy the cow although he has already had the milk for free;* but have we not been called to so much more?

If you are a married person reading this book, I pray for your marriage's success. Even if you began with the wrong objective, it is my desire that you and your spouse refocus your attention and allow the Lord to help you live a successful and enriching life together. If however you are single, then this is just for you. Do not allow personal misconceptions or those belonging to others lead you down a path of error. Instead, learn and accept that God, who created marriage, has a handle on what is best in the execution of it. By the time you read to the final page, I pray that God's spirit would have spoken to you and shown you what, if any, changes you need to make in order to complete His purpose in your life. There can be joy in singleness once you realize that contentment of any depth will not be determined by your situation but by the way you choose to handle that situation. As you complete each chapter, there are three things I implore you to do:

1. Pray – ask God to help you identify the way this material in any way relates to you and ask for his help in strengthening your resolve or in making the changes as necessary. Be honest with yourself and remember that God knows it all anyway so you may as well be honest with him too.

2. In the journal spaces that follow, write down specific actions you may need to take in order to make whatever adjustments He has revealed to you.

3. Pray – thank God for opening your eyes, request the strength to follow through for yourself and for the others who like you must make adjustments to live meaningful, God-oriented single lives.

1 Single and Happy ...Paradox?

"Those who marry will face many troubles in this life"

1 Corinthians 7: 28 (NIV)

As an opening to one of his sermons on being the spirit filled single, my pastor read a list titled *The Good Side of Singlehood,* something he had come across on the internet but did not know the original writer of. According to this writer, singlehood does have a few pluses that seem to escape the sight of many:

- I can squeeze the toothpaste in the middle, back, front – anywhere on the tube I want!
- I don't have to explain why I am late and I am always late
- I only have to make ½ of the bed
- I don't have to endure cold feet against my leg
- I don't have to verify that the toilet seat is down before sitting
- I can drink directly out of the milk carton
- I don't have to go on a diet to support his efforts
- I can run the air conditioner longer without being reminded what it costs
- I can choose the TV station on Monday night

- I don't have to pretend to like her parents
- I can belch after every meal

Obviously this writer's aim was to generate humor. Wit aside, singleness does have its benefits; but for those who name the name of Christ, it also has added responsibility.

First Things First

Two weeks prior to my twenty-fifth birthday I found myself in a depressive slump. I had surveyed my life and concluded that I had not accomplished quite a number of the goals I had set for myself. Incidentally, two of those included marriage and motherhood, having two, possibly three, children by the time I was thirty. At twenty-five I was not dating anyone seriously and every relationship that seemed to *fit my bill* had turned unsuccessful so it was unlikely that my target would be reached. I now laugh (hysterically too) at that because I know how unprepared I had been to handle the kind of life I craved. My views on many things have changed so radically; and many of my desires of that time have evolved or matured, now seeming foolish and insignificant. Prior to that birthday however, I remember feeling inadequate and asking God to show me what was wrong with me. Why had I failed at attracting a good, godly man who would make my life make sense? Though I loved and trusted the Lord, this trust was obviously not as complete as I had thought and I had lived with the misconception that happiness was wrapped up in my circumstances; I believed that my life was incomplete and unhappy because I did not have these things I wanted.

There is colossal irony in the fact that many believers, like me back then, trust God for their eternal salvation yet prevent him from featuring in much of the other aspects of their lives. It was in that state that I began to cry out to the Lord. I felt lonely and unfulfilled. Friends could not meet the physical need a husband could, and though God is a *"friend who sticks closer than a brother"*[4] I could not see, touch, or audibly hear Him. Because I did not know what else to do I poured out my soul to

[4] Proverbs 18:24 (NIV)

God, telling him exactly how I was feeling and asking him to intervene.

The first and most important thing that will enrich any life is a commitment to Jesus Christ. Though I did not appreciate it then, it was my commitment to Jesus, through salvation, that allowed me to realize I could turn and cry to Him in this very distressing time. Later, it would be a wholehearted commitment to fulfilling *His* purposes in my life that would cause a total transformation in me: a transformation whereby I re-channeled my focus and desire to please God, not self. Had I not had that moment of introspection, I would not have realized that I had been living my life in a self-centered way.

Too often believers try to fit God's plans around their personal schedules and then run to God for him to put His stamp of approval on their plans, when it should be vice versa. My life had been self consumed. I had had no intention to stop attending church or participating in the activities there, my aspirations however, remotely stemmed from a desire to fulfill God's mandate for my life. Ashamedly, I was earth centered: the career, the house, the car, the family, had become my focus and goal in all that I did. None of these things in and of themselves are sinful, but when they take the place of an individual's desire to please God they cause a spiritual problem.

God wants an intimate relationship with every person on this planet. When he created Adam and Eve, the first man and woman, and placed them in perfect Eden, God *"… [walked] in the garden in the cool of the day…"*[5] He did not put them in the garden and leave them there, he sought to have fellowship with them. After sin, he sent Jesus to die for mankind's sin, so that he could restore the relationship that Adam and Eve's disobedience had severed and prove that He was not only concerned with creating us but also loving us.

When marriage becomes a single individual's central focus, it usually results in that person's distraction from God and preoccupation with a worldly view because he/she has allowed their immediate desires to supersede God's purpose. Let's say God has not called an individual to a life of singleness. How

---

[5] Genesis 3:8 (NKJV)

then does that individual live *until* he/she is married? Is that person going to be less happy until then? The single life cannot be less happy than a married one since God did not create us only to be married (regardless of the number of years that pass before an individual is married); yet we are brought up believing the course of our lives is to grow up, go to school, become adults, marry, procreate, grow old then die. In fact many parents are disappointed when their children do not marry. Females in particular face a social scourge if they do not become wives and mothers, hence the term "old maid".

Unfortunately when some persons make the decision to marry, many do not seek God's direction; "he/she loves me, I love him/her" is too often the determining factors when, as believers, our plans should stem from a "what does God want?" attitude. I know that such a declaration is more easily said than done but it is certainly not impossible. Too many Christians undermine the power of the Holy Spirit and his ability to truly guide us. We are sometimes fearful of even asking for His intervention lest we be led where we believe that we do not want to go. To recognize however that God has not given the believer a spirit of fear and that this confidence should be tapped into at every point of our lives, should be the Christian's goal. James 5:17 always challenges me because of its reference to Elijah's mortality yet ability to harness God's power through prayer. I am inclined to believe that many 21st Century Christians are spiritually weaker because of our lack of prayer and a belief that "*we've got this*." Our prayer lives are more often than not jumpstarted only after our plans have gone awry.

<u>'No Spouse?'</u> (Gasp)

Society too does not seem to suggest that singleness is even a favorable state of being. In fact, it is often portrayed as some sort of intermediary; and persons who never marry are never quite initiated into adulthood. Those who marry later in life are sometimes pitied and sighs of relief are breathed when they *finally escape* the *humdrum* of the single life.

One of the biggest mistakes most married friends make is to assume all their single friends want them to *fix 'em up*, i.e. help them find a mate. I cannot recall the number of offers I have received (some from well meaning friends) to *find a husband for me* or the suggestions that 'so and so' would be *perfect* for me. Of course, there are single folk who do not mind the idea of their friends doing the match making, and so there is no real harm in getting the sticks together for a possible fire to be ignited. I am also certain there have been many successful relationships birthed from 'blind dates' and other such *orchestrations*. I believe however there is a misconception that being single is a defect of some kind. In the same way some people have a college education and some do not, some people get married and some do not. Does a doctorate degree guarantee a successful or lucrative career or the lack thereof mean a life of poverty? Why then do some people propagate the idea that you are unhappy or incomplete until…?

We are trained it seems to believe that refusing to marry speaks to a deficiency in our social and relational attitudes, *"You are selfish. How can you not want to be married?" or "What's wrong with you?" or still, "You're not bad looking, how come you aren't married?"* Statistics show however that divorce rates, even among Christians, are increasingly high. Why are marriages, even Christian ones, not passing the tests of difficult times? Perhaps it is because too many of us have bought into a philosophy of "happiness by circumstance", and like fame and money, marriage is seen as a means to an end – the happiness end. Therefore if life's occurrences do not yield that expected feeling, then many are ready to call it quits.

Oftentimes one's culture and social circles may lead an individual into thinking that their being single is a result of something they are/are not doing. Instead of pining for a spouse, such persons will do well to seek to develop their relationships with God, develop themselves as individuals, and build lasting and meaningful relationships with some of those with whom they come in contact. Singleness does not mean solitude. Let me hasten to add my wholehearted belief that God created us for community and relationships. It is in fact the meaningful relationships the single person will form that will help him/ her get through the difficult and sometimes lonely moments.

By the testimony of many, I agree that marriage can be an enriching experience. My parents have been married for close to forty years, and though very few children are privy to the actual marital difficulties their parents may experience, their union has for me been that perennial model of what a Christian union should resemble. Similarly however, marriage can be torturous and disappointing if it is entered into lightly and the foundations are not solid enough to sustain life beyond the *honeymoon stage.*

Singly Loose

I have had a few, what may be casually termed intimate relationships with men, some of whom even professed to know the Lord. I had however come up short and empty because I had desired a fulfillment that could not be found in those relationships. Where then was the happiness that I was seeking so fiercely? Did it not lie in the family I was *supposed* to have? Ignorance is a wall less prison, but until there is the acceptance and acknowledgment of God's supreme power and control of every aspect of our lives, even the most educated can become trapped in it. The Apostle Paul's words of 1 Corinthians 7 are often met with much disdain and cynicism, yet from Paul's words, it is clear to me that there are some people whom God has designed to desire marriage as much as there are those who have been designed not to. As Paul expounds in 1 Corinthians 7:7 however, singleness of a permanent nature, is a giftedness that, though not all will have, is no way a status that ought to be pitied or ridiculed. Whatever objectives God has by so doing, lie in the fact that there are some things he desires that we accomplish that will not be as selflessly executed by those who are married. Such objectives will similarly be hampered however if that life is spent wishing "*what if?*"

There is the idea propagated by popular media that singleness is that period for experimentation, sexual freedom and playing the field; after all if one is not restricted to the rules and regulations of marriage why not 'do as you feel'? Reality television programs have become the order of the day, and there is a seeming unlimited variety of options for both male and female singles that seek a mate, whether their relationship goal is long or short term. Needless to say, the polar morals between what is portrayed on these programs and those that God intended for his creation have muddied the rules for some, with the former becoming accepted as the norm.

Although the aspects of dating, marriage and parenting are important in their own respects, they exist only as part of a bigger, an even more significant realm of things. Real life is centered by God. Married or single, life will have pockets of emptiness without Him. Married or single, life will be fulfilling and complete *with* Him. An individual only needs to reflect on any one thing he/she may have desired at one time. I have prayed "if only I could finish paying my student loans", "if only I made more money", "if only I had my own car", and the list goes on. Having achieved these and other things, I have noticed that the satisfaction was but temporary, it faded after I had grown accustomed to whatever it is that I had desired at the time. If I then grew tired of my acquisitions, then true happiness could never lie in what I could physically obtain.

All is Vanity... Except

"And it all begins with You,

The secret of life is walking closer to the truth

Even the mountains bow to You

The stars are ornaments in the sky, they testify

That it all begins with You"

Jody Wately (1991)

Where then does true happiness lie? Solomon acknowledged that the whole duty of man was to fear God.[6] This era has advanced in technology, production, travel, discoveries et cetera. Though some seemed impossible only a generation or two ago, Scripture posits that "*there is nothing new under the sun*"[7] People are still the same. Our toys have evolved but our needs have not changed. Solomon searched for the meaning of life, a meaning which he did not find in all his riches, regality or many relationships. The wisest man who ever lived discovered that life's meaning was bound in a

[6] Ecclesiastes 12:13 (NIV)

[7] Ecclesiastes 1:9 (NIV)

relationship with God and nothing else. That is where it begins. All the other gadgets will only be added to complement the primary focus of our lives. This is why I propose that the person who is unhappy *because* he/she is single has not yet discovered the real reason God has placed him/her on this planet. When one begins to enjoy the Lord, happiness in everything else is the natural result.

Depending on a being that cannot be physically seen or touched to harness one's happiness goes against what is deemed normal. However whether an individual chooses to acknowledge this idea or not, we have all been made with a vacuum, one that may be referred to as a God – shaped vacuum; and attempting to fill this void with anything else will result in a lifetime of endless searching. History reiterates man's need for a spiritual relationship, and when he does not understand who God is man creates gods to fill this void. Unfortunately, that god sometimes comes in the form of a man or a woman, a relationship. The damning result is, because of our human inadequacies we fail at truly satisfying our happiness need in a relationship.

The institution of marriage must be regarded as one aspect of community, and although it is an important step towards ultimate intimacy between men and women, we must be reminded that God has not called us all to be married. His objectives go beyond the pleasurable feelings we seek; and in order to achieve these we, his soldiers, ought to be mentally and spiritually prepared for the tasks he has outlined for us. Since marriage is only one aspect of community, one aspect of relationships, it therefore should not become the primary goal for the single person's life. If marriage becomes the goal in life what happens after this has been *achieved*? Or what if it is never *achieved* does this render the life meaningless? One of my purposes here is to speak to the fact that God desires to use single persons now.

> *"An unmarried man is concerned about the Lord's affairs – how he can please the Lord. But a married man is concerned about the affairs of this world – how he can please his wife and his interests are divided. An unmarried woman or virgin is concerned about the Lord's affairs: Her aim is to be devoted to the Lord in body*

and spirit. But the married woman is concerned about the affairs of this world – how she can please her husband."

I Corinthians 7: 32-34

Was the Apostle Paul daring to suggest that married people are less dedicated Christians? By all means no! On the contrary he was illustrating that because the institution of marriage is such an important one, married persons must devote time to building and supporting their families. It is to some degree ironic that Scriptural admonition regarding marriage would be the absolute opposite of what most people think, well at least those of us who are not married. The fairytales have misled us. They all end with the *"... and they all lived happily ever after"* line, blinding most of us to the reality of life after the guests and bridal party go home, we change clothes and the bills begin to pile up. To get marriage to work, the parties have to *work.* The Scriptural quote that headlines this chapter reiterates the fact that the concerns of marriage go way beyond how many tiers we will have on the wedding cake. It is little wonder therefore that God expects the parties' ability to commit to duties outside of the home to be less. Single persons who do not have this concern can then contribute to the ministry in a way married people cannot. The bottom line is that all are working for the fulfillment of God's overall purpose.

In all fairness it will be tempting to feel some inadequacy when many of the friends or other people you grew up with begin to marry and have families of their own. However to assume that being single necessarily points to a failure in your life goes contrary to what we have been discussing thus far. Scripture proves it and history echoes that proof. Happiness can be acquired even in the midst of being single once we do not take our cues from a world that tries to suggest otherwise. Until a person recognizes his/her worth to Christ, the pursuit of meaningful happiness will continue. Albeit some search for it in other things, the point is that outside of Christ it will not be found; and it most certainly will not be obtained by joining one's self to another.

One's life does not begin *after* finding that proverbial *right person.* Many believe there is a void in their lives that this person will fill. They live waiting and so do not enjoy life to the fullest. I have often heard spouses speak of their "better half". Though many do so in jest, it is something worth considering. Are we emotional half persons until we meet others to *complete* us? Among the most popular ideas of the concept of a soul mate is the Greek mythological belief that the Greek god, Zeus, had split humans (who originally had four arms and legs with a single head that had two faces) down the middle; thus forcing us to spend our lifetimes in search of that other half for completion. Scripture however shows us that there were no such alterations after God had created male and female[8] and I believe He wants to use whole persons now. In fact, those who do marry will find that their marriages will work better if they enter with the mindset that their mates complement and not complete their lives. Only God can truly do that.

[8] Genesis 1:27,31

Key Reminder:

Your happiness does not lie in a situation, but in a relationship with Christ

What does this mean for me?

2- Lonely Times

"Lonely days, Lonely nights, where would I be without my woman?"

Bee gees (1975)

My biggest struggle with being single is related to sexual activity (or rather the lack thereof). How does a Christian single person deal with the fact that there are certain levels of intimacy that are prohibited unless he/she is married? I remember once being asked by a friend what I did to combat those natural sexual desires. This is a battle that must be fought in the heart and mind before it can be won in the physical. How then have I dealt with the innate desire for sexual relations? I will immediately admit that initially it was a serious fight to quiet those urges though I held fast to the scriptural instruction to avoid sexual immorality. But how can anyone rein in these sexual urges that occasionally seem uncontrollable? I asked God to quell my sexual desires until I had the appropriate avenue, through marriage, for it to be unleashed. Such a decision was more difficult than it sounds, difficult but not impossible. Only salvation is instant, and even then, one has much to do in order to develop the Christ likeness that God desires in all his children.

Abracadabra…NOT

The instant transformation that I was hoping for did not happen. I was faced with constant temptation and repeated failure. Though I did not succumb to the physical sexual act I stumbled repeatedly in thought, and according to Scripture, that was just as bad:

"But I tell you that anyone who looks at a woman lustfully has already committed adultery with her in his heart"[9]

Naturally the passage equally applies to a woman looking on a man. The more I pressed however, was the more I realized that God could truly reign in me. I also recognized and acknowledged that my issues were not unique to me:

There hath no temptation taken [me] but such as is common to man, but God is faithful and will not Suffer [me] to be tempted above that which [I am] able, But will with the temptation make a way of escape that [I] will be able to bear it.[10]

In the same way God allows me to face these testing situations, He also prepares a way for me

---

[9] Matthew 5: 28 (NIV)

[10] I Corinthians 10:13 (KJV)

to get out of them. The trick is to be in the frame of mind to recognize what escape route he has set up for me.

If you are familiar with Old Testament Scripture, then your thoughts may almost immediately flash to Joseph, who in Genesis 39 had to deal with the temptation of resisting his boss' wife who repeatedly threw herself at him. This young man 'gave up' the opportunity to sleep with the wife of one of the most powerful men in Egypt, not because he was afraid of being caught, but because he saw his actions in direct violation of what God would want.[11] Ironically, his refusal resulted in him being thrown in prison! How unfair, we may think; but God had a bigger purpose to achieve through Joseph's imprisonment. Joseph saw his "way of escape", and though the initial repercussions were not favorable, God was pleased and Joseph's later successes proved that.[12] These are the thoughts that have helped to strengthen me in my weakest moments. The devoted believer must accept that God's purpose supersedes

[11] Genesis 39:9

[12] Genesis 39: 2 – 5; 21 – 23; 41: 39 - 41

his/her immediate feelings of bliss; and although God does desire that we do experience some pleasure now, Earth is not to be confused with Heaven. As difficult as it may be to wrap our heads around the idea that *bad* things will happen, Christ has overcome the world[13] and our discomfort is temporary.

While learning to combat the desire of instant gratification, which more often than not will cause us to overlook God's "way of escape" for us; we may become tempted, as I was, to battle sexual urges by working constantly. Since I was always busy with programs and activities I thought I would not have the time to be even thinking about sex. I was however only successful in sapping practically every ounce of energy I had because when I occasionally had some *down time* when there was nothing to capture my attention; my 'dragon' raised its ugly head. Since I had not learnt to master these urges, my thoughts became overpowered and before I knew what was happening I was back at square one.

[13] John 16:33

In and of personal strength, I would never condemn Christian brothers and sisters who have repeatedly been overpowered by their sexual urges. Undoubtedly many continue in secret, others mother/father children, still others allow this to be the reason they turn away from close fellowship with God. Scripture does point out however that sexual immorality is something God deals with very severely and 1 Corinthians 6:18, among many other scripture passages, highlights that believers are held to a high standard:

> *"Flee sexual immorality. All other sins a man commits are outside his body, but he who sins sexually sins against his own body" (NIV)*

Since the body of the believer is God's temple, then there is a serious responsibility to take care of that temple in a way that brings honor to God. I have been to the proverbial *edge* on too many occasions, and had it not been for the realization that my desires for romance were included in all my "cares", [14] I would no doubt have plummeted a long time ago. I embarked on what I now term a soul searching; seeking God's assistance in dealing with this natural need because I was single. Though I was comfortable dating casually, I know I wasn't interested in being married at this time, and getting married in order to legitimize my desire for sex would not only result in my cheating myself, but also that unlucky man, of a good and satisfying marriage.

Coping 101

It was then that the Holy Spirit directed me to establish some boundaries for my life. My decisions have sometimes been met with raised eyebrows and other looks of disbelief but I have quickly learned to accept that if this was something I struggled with, then I would have to make the calls that would help me, regardless of what anyone thought. The fear of giving off an

[14] I Peter 5:7

air of 'super spirituality' has sometimes quieted me when I recognize others with similar needs, I remember viewing other persons' decisions in that manner until I was at the stage of my life where I had to make such tough calls. When pleasing God really becomes important to an individual, they will challenge themselves by doing the things that everyone else deems ridiculous. Naturally perfection will never be possible in this life, but that should not stop us from seeking after it and aiming to get as close as is humanly possible. Galatians 5:16 – 26 is an excellent 'How To' manual with regard to living as a believer. In order to achieve success over sin a person must be ready to give themself over to the control of God's spirit.

The first step I took in dealing with those lonely times was self examination. In what way(s) was the way I conducted my life encouraging/ planting seed for these desires to feed on? I examined what I viewed on television, read, listened to, conversations I participated in et cetera; and I saw how aspects of these different things could contribute to the sort of life I was trying to escape. Whatever is inside of an individual is what will come out.

The importance of what we take in is something that cannot be approached lightly. In order to achieve what is beyond the ordinary, then one must be ready to act in a manner that exceeds what is ordinary and that is what 1 Corinthians 6:12 encouraged me to do "*Everything is permissible for me but not everything is beneficial*". There were some things that needed to be weeded from my life not because they were wrong per say, but because they offered no help in my desire for spiritual growth. I avoided deliberately listening to secular songs that were predominantly focused on sex or on immoral relationships. I also extended that scrutiny to my selection of the movies I watched at the theatre, on local cable television or on DVDs I purchased. Neither did my choice of literature include romance novels. Being what may be loosely termed a *fun* person I had initially seen nothing wrong with being *harmlessly* flirtatious, but that was behavior that also required stemming. I even promised myself that the next gentleman I would romantically kiss would be the man I am marrying when the officiating minister said "*you may now kiss the bride*".

These decisions seemed extreme even to my own thoughts, and I backpedaled and second guessed myself as to whether such extreme measures were actually necessary. Admittedly, there have been occasional slip-ups, but I am determined that what I want to achieve is greater than a few moments of discomfort. Each of these decisions takes a daily reaffirmation and though my goals are more easily achieved on some days, others are a definite struggle. The dates too are fewer now since my criteria is more strictly adhered to and pleasing God trumps anything else as *"to obey is better than sacrifice"*[15]

My second step involved redirection. Maybe it is a 'chick' thing, or my right brain was perhaps in overdrive, or I may just have had too much time on my hands; but I would dare to assume that even occasionally, every person reading this book has drifted into the realm of daydreams. I often caught myself creating scenarios of the kind of man I wanted to marry and building a story in my mind of our lives together, every aspect of it. When those times

---

[15] 1 Samuel 15:22 (KJV)

would come I would begin to refocus my attention, keeping prayer of course a central factor. After a while these kinds of daydreams were reduced; but that too is a daily decision. There is no quick fix to any situation that involves spiritual growth. Christ admonished the need for daily commitment to Him;[16] and as physical food is required daily for one's strength, spiritual regeneration requires repeated commitment to one's purpose.

If you have ever been watching television late at night, even regular cable television, you may have seen commercials with beautiful girls inviting persons to call for casual and flirtatious conversations. A few even suggested that face to face meetings were possible if desired. The hook was that calling for these conversations was purely for *fun* since not all persons are looking for committed relationships. Perchance my criticism is heightened because this is a subject of particular interest to me; but these commercials imply that phone sex is seen as a viable alternative to the commitment of a marriage and nothing is wrong since callers may

[16] St. Luke 9: 23 - 25

only be talking. In the same vein is the attitude of having friends with benefits which just basically means sex is available and no *strings* of commitment are attached. Therefore the idea is suggested that although an individual may not desire marriage, there are so many options available that he/she can have all the physical benefits of one without the emotional and I dare mention spiritual requirements of it. I feel compelled to mention this because the media is often guilty of purporting these ideas as though they are practical means of dealing with singleness. Since Christians like everyone else, are consumers of media, it is very important that we guard our minds against becoming sympathetic towards this kind of attitude/ lifestyle.

It is essential to understand that it is natural to crave affection; however since the God who created us with these desires also made some stipulations as to how we go about displaying these affections for others, it is necessary then for those who claim to serve him to act according to the guidelines that Scripture has outlined. It is amazing that many of us are quick to ask *"how far can I go without stepping over the line into the realm of sin?"* Instead of trying to walk as far away as possible, we look for ways to tiptoe around God's instructions and to somehow justify our actions later. But what can we do now? How does the single man or woman conquer his/her God-given desires? I have discovered that those who are single, whether because it is the current stage of their lives or because they are persuaded of a spiritual call to singleness, have a responsibility to understand their roles. Similar to the roles of a husband or a wife, God has some expectations of single folk. Once these roles are fulfilled then we will live the meaningful lives that many too often believe will be achieved only *after* they become husbands or wives.

Reference has already been made to the Apostle Paul's guidelines concerning attitudes to singleness in 1 Corinthians 7. It obviously calls for a shift in focus, one of a God-view instead of a world-view. Until this is achieved we will continue to struggle with the idea of singleness since our perspectives will be hazed by what the world expects of us. When we become cognizant of the responsibility we have as believers, that is our responsibility to honor God,[17] then our desires will change and we will not allow ourselves to become subject to the dictates of this world. Since our singleness, as Paul purports, allows us the freedom to serve God more effectively, believers who are determined to live lives that first please Him will seek to maximize the opportunity that being single affords.

Undoubtedly what is being recommended here will be highly unpopular because most of us have become accustomed to the school of thought that involves pleasing ourselves. The earlier reference to Galatians 5, along with Romans 12: 1-2, Colossians 3:2 and countless others, indicate that the Christian's mandate has nothing to do with pleasing ourselves. Interestingly, once our focuses change to ones that are primarily focused on pleasing God through our commitment to him, we get fulfillment and the lonely days and nights will become fewer, even if marriage does not change the landscape of our lives.

---

[17] I Corinthians 6:20

Key Reminder: 

Dealing with the seeming lonely times becomes easier when single individuals change their perspectives

What does this mean for me?

Who Are You?

Chameleon: "a variable or inconsistent person"
©Oxford University Press 1995

Perhaps originating from the small lizard that has the distinguishing ability to adjust its color, presumably in its attempt to protect itself from danger, the term chameleon is often used to describe persons who are frequently changing. In his *1917 "The Love Song of J. Alfred Prufrock"* T.S Eliot's now famous line we *"prepare a face to meet the faces that we meet"* suggests that at some time or another, every individual will conceal some aspect of him/herself.

The chameleonic characteristic, to which I now refer however, has little to do with being discreet. It instead refers to an unawareness of self and a decision to be whomever the latest fad or current love interest dictates that you be. If I change my hair or buy a new outfit it is sometimes interpreted by casual observers that I am "looking out," i.e. on the prowl for a suitor. Is there anything wrong with ensuring that you are attractively put together? Certainly not! However something is definitely wrong with doing the aforementioned things *in order to* seek attention or doing things outside of your character because it is believed that you will please onlookers. It is a natural, animal instinct to seek to attract the opposite sex,

> *"All animals have a different way of attracting a mate - some animals use a special call, or a display of bright colors or strength, or weird dance, or a display of affection such as licking. There is also a special scent that some females secrete when on heat, which attracts the male to them, and is the same sort of thing that*

> *males produce when marking their territory..."* [18]

Humans likewise have a tendency to do the same things; and oftentimes the perfume, the makeup, the muscles, the tattoos are all in a bid to garner the attention of the opposite sex; but since we were made only a "*little lower than the angels*"[19] I do believe we have a bit more control over the instinct that inordinately governs the animal kingdom. When we start with loving and appreciating ourselves as God intended then fulfillment and self actualization will not stem from a false sense of security that comes from our appearances or what others believe about us. It will instead be derived from an internal sense of confidence that comes from understanding and accepting that even in the midst of seeming inadequacies our existence is not happenstance; and even the very color of our eyes or the places we were born were by specific design.

---

[18] http://wiki.answers.com/Q/What_do_animals_do_to_attract_other_animals

[19] Hebrews 2: 7 (KJV)

Fearfully and Wonderfully Made

Before I grew to appreciate and love myself, I sought affirmation from the people around me, especially those of the opposite sex. The interesting thing is, though this affirmation was received, I often questioned whether the displayed affection was genuine. It was as though I doubted whether or not I was worthy to gain those persons' approval, and quite readily believed they pretended for personal gain. In retrospect, I realize that this attitude was an act of projection. Because my own reasons for dating hinged on what I could get out of a relationship and not what I would bring to it, I distrusted the intentions of those around me. As far as a relationship was concerned, I sought someone who could ensure some sort of prestige; whether because of his financial or social position, or because of educational or athletic accomplishments. This kind of attitude fed my insecurities because when I met persons who I believed did not meet my expectations, I then thought that they desired to use me in the same why I was searching for a *"trophy date"*.

These insecurities ruined not only my relationships but my general view of people.

This process of self acceptance and self love has been a long and sometimes tedious journey, but I have arrived at the place where I am now because of my relationship with the Lord Jesus. Men and women alike are plagued with insecurities. We fear what people will think about our looks, our achievements, even our faults, and that we will never measure up because of a defect that we identify in ourselves. This hurdle cannot be surmounted until we first begin with what God thinks about us. When we recognize our own worth, then the desire to find absolution in another immediately dissipates. I mourn for those who have used jobs, education, leisure activities, even marriage as a means of filling the void left by insecurity; because any satisfaction they gain is temporary. As soon as the feeling of utopia ends, their search will continue.

Becoming who God wants you to be works in tandem with becoming your own person. The media and popular opinion have their own take on who individuals are supposed to be; and this makes it easy to become sidetracked by what is popularly considered desirable. Advertisers thrive on our insecurities in order to make their products attractive. How else can you be a part of the "in crowd" go to the "best schools" have the "coveted attention" or land the "right jobs" unless you buy into whatever is being marketed? While our society is structured to accommodate this viewpoint, self worth cannot be truly determined by anything other than what the Creator has said. This is why I believe the most important step towards self discovery and enrichment in life is commitment to Jesus Christ. Until this is done, trying to believe what God thinks about you may be somewhat difficult since He who said you were *"fearfully and wonderfully made"*[20] also said *"[you were] sinful at birth, sinful from the time your mother conceived [you]"*[21]. Should an individual decide to be honest with himself then an acknowledgement of his spiritual state is paramount.

This principle works both ways. If I accept that I am a sinner and it is only God who can change me, then all the good things He says about me are also true. I am who God says I am. Some of my favorite portions of Scripture are the ones that speak of God's concern for those

[20] Psalm 139:14 (NIV)
[21] Psalm 52:5 (NIV)

who trust Him. *"Delight yourself* ***in the Lord*** *and He will give you the desire of your heart."*[22] *"Do not worry about your life... But seek first the kingdom of God and his righteousness, and all these things shall be added to you.*[23] Matthew's gospel specifically names the provision of clothes and food as a frequent point of worry for many but the passage also says "your life" so I believe all that is connected to our lives is of God's concern. If He cares enough to name stars and number the hairs on our heads,[24] then He is surely concerned about the things that make us happy.

Once an individual is in tune with God and what he wants, then this life, which lines up with God, is less likely to be chameleonic and more likely to be successful. We were created by and for God, and as such pleasing him should be the first order of the day. Naturally once He is pleased we will be pleased.[25] When an individual's sense of who he/ she is has been developed, then should that person decide to start a romantic relationship, it less likely that

---

[22] Psalm 37:4 (NIV)
[23] Matthew 6:25,33 (NKJV)
[24] Matthew 10:30
[25] Psalm 37:4

character surprises will appear later down in the relationship as there were few misconceptions to begin with. There is a popular Caribbean saying, *"see mi and come live with mi a two different thing"*. It basically suggests that persons have a tendency to hide their true characters because what is seen from afar is entirely different from the reality of what is exposed when the individuals are more closely connected. This saying is meant to "justify" why many persons opt to live with their romantic interests prior to marrying them in order to test the waters and see if they could get along when they must share the same space. In speaking of the now Duke and Duchess of Cambridge, William and Kate's decision to live together prior to their April 2011 marriage, one writer's response suggests that the modernization of cultures equates with a right to disregard God's directives, *"If Her Majesty's royal subjects are aghast at the disclosure that William and Kate have been cohabiting, they haven't shown it.* ***But then again, it is 2010****"*[26], further highlighting the fact that it behooves Christians to take their cues from the Bible and

[26] http://today.msnbc.msn.com/id/40253368/ns/today-today_people/t/royal-shack-up-kate-william-moved-months-ago

not the shifting tide of culture. It was never God's intention for us to have a trial run or he would not have spoken so strongly against sexual impurity, and the sanctity of sexual relations within the bounds of marriage. This therefore brings me full circle to the point of being true to self; but before individuals can be true to self they must know themselves.

There are hundreds of self-help manuals available that teach some aspect of self discovery and love. Only the ones that start with the Biblical take however, gain any merit in my eyes. How else does one solve the problems of something unless the manual created by the maker is examined or studied? Controversial rap artist Eminem shouted *"I am whatever you say I am, if I wasn't then why would you say I am?"* How wrong to declare to be what others, and not God, says you are. What is the basis for another's judgment of you? Knowing and defining yourself is crucial to understanding what, if any, romantic relationships should be pursued.

I am always interested in what individuals have to say concerning romantic relationships since it is such a major aspect of most of our lives. Among the top ten things men wanted in a woman according to A. K Boyle's October 19, 2006 internet blog is the women's knowledge of and willingness to ask for what she wants as well as a woman's willingness to make up her own mind and have a degree of self-sufficiency "*Independence is strong and attractive, and it's a plus when he knows you're autonomous enough to be on your own.*"[27] Sheri and Bob Stritof in their blog of what wives want from husbands listed a desire that men take care of themselves, *"Many men are notorious for not taking care of themselves when it comes to health issues. This isn't fair to your wife. She is your lover not your mother"*[28] once again highlighting the fact that both men and women seem most interested in *not* having their lives consumed by the other. This ability to take care of self does not materialize overnight, it must stem from a decision to cultivate a personality of one's own regardless of what is construed to be what a romantic interest will desire. Not only does pretending make one unhappy, but

[27] http://blog.californiapsychics.com/blog/2006/10/10-things-men-want-in-a-woman.html

[28] http://marriage.about.com/od/marriagetoolbox/tp/wiveswant.htm

pretending can only last for a short while and given time the true character will be revealed.

Key Reminder:

Knowing who you are as God has created you must occur in order for a happy single life to be realized

What does this mean for me?

4 - Moving On

I fell in love when I was fifteen years old. The guy was someone I had known for a few years because of the relationship my parents had with his. However we lived in different towns and that year was the first time I ever had extended contact with him via the yearly summer camp that both our churches participated in. He was dating someone at the time so I nursed my crush from afar. It would be about five years later when there seemed to be some glimmer of hope for me. By then, although his previous relationship had ended, he was studying overseas and that was what now hampered any possibility of the development of a serious relationship between him and me. Nevertheless, we shared lots of emails and had a few phone conversations and my heart was taken… actually I had given it up; apparently it had not been received. Because I was uncertain of his feelings for me I was too afraid to let on that what I felt went beyond a mere friendship though I now believe my actions could not have been more obvious. When he had completed his studies and returned home I was elated. Our friendship had developed, we spent more time together and it was certain, in my own mind that is, that he was the one my father would pass my hand over to as I would very soon grace the aisle of a church, beautifully clad in white.

I still remember the night he introduced me to a young lady whom he had recently met and she had asked him out, I still remember when, almost a year later, he told me he would be married in the spring. For years following I berated myself for not being proactive enough and taking the initiative that woman had. Now however, that memory comes with no pain, no hatred for the woman I once envied and believed had stolen my one chance for happiness. It took several years for me to be delivered from this hurt and to confront the reasons for the way I felt. Not only had I been angry at God since I had prayed long and hard for Him to allow me to have this man; but in the years following, every guy I dated was measured against this man who had seemed to be the yin to my yang. Acknowledging his rejection is something I struggled to deal with; and because of this my life was at a standstill for several years. Even the reminder of God's undeniable acceptance of who I was did very little to quell the hurt I experienced.

As I have grown older and also matured spiritually; I have come to the realization that in order to truly serve the Lord there must be a complete sense of abandonment of self. Scoffers often see such an attitude as an attempt to "cop out" of responsibility. It was the German economist and Communist political philosopher, Karl Marx, who said *"...religion is the opiate of the people..."*[29] but to suggest that true religion merely numbs pain instead of offers solutions for the healing of the situation, is evidence that Marx only saw a *type* of religion where people perhaps lost themselves in religious practices, failing to yield their will to God's control. I

[29] http://www.phrases.org.uk/meanings/300700.html

have seen in my own life and heard the testimonies of many others as to the ease with which humans opt to solve their problems by themselves, turning to God only as the ultimate resort. To in fact surrender to someone outside of ourselves, especially outside of our complete understanding therefore goes beyond a natural inclination or a mere *opiate.* Instead it takes a conscious decision, one naturally against our will to yield, especially when it seems that God's responses are slow in coming or what His Spirit and Word direct us to do go contrary to our desires.

Once again I refer to God's *big picture.* Regardless of the number of times I have read or heard the Book of Job preached I am flabbergasted by Job's faith. Certainly because he was human and capable of hurt, Job cried out in his pain, even wishing he was never born,[30] yet his faith was constant[31]. His faith was certainly not a balm at this time. His decision to trust God, even to reprimand his wife for her suggestion that he curse God,[32] came out of an understanding that although he could not see or

---

[30] Job 3:1-13

[31] Job 13: 15;19: 25-27; 23:10

[32] Job 2:9

understand it God had a grand scheme, a *big picture*. His success during his testing resulted in him receiving even more than he had before.[33]

I will hasten to add that trust/faith in God must not be something we do solely in hope of material gain. God is not a genie; and since He can read our thoughts anyway, we are not able to trick Him, so such actions are fruitless and never to our benefit. When an individual decides to *"seek first the kingdom of God,"*[34] he/she is required to exercise an unusual faith which often results in their desires being altered since their heart begins to crave after what God wants more than what they want. In fact, as the author of Hebrews clearly outlines in Chapter 11:39, sometimes we make the tough choices, do the right things and nothing great happens to us. That is why faith involves believing in what you cannot see.[35] Romantic relationships prove to be no exception. Allowing God to be the Most Valuable Player (MVP) of your life, instead of a mere spectator will mean you will permit Him to play a part in this area of your life as well. In order to move on, an individual must be willing

---

[33] Job 42:12 - 17

[34] Matthew 6:33 (KJV)

[35] Hebrews 11:1

to let go – to release every aspect of that relationship to God, believing that as He cared enough to die for you, He cares enough to govern your life's plan. There will be a number of times God's *big picture* will make no sense to us; but the testimonies of those before us that have been recorded in Scripture undeniably point to a God who vindicates, provides and punishes where necessary.

What does all this have to do with living singly? It means that God can be trusted. He is on His own schedule and when an individual decides to yield his/her entire life to Him that path is immediately certain - not smooth, but certain. The image of a blind man being carefully led across an unfamiliar street pops into mind as a reflection of God's hands in an individual's life. The guide sees the pitfalls, he sees the obstacles and he sees the smoothest parts. Similarly God's leading will be dependent on what He wants to achieve in our lives. To move on from past hurt or disappointment is a mark that we believe our steps are being ordered by a master designer who is able to help us pick up the pieces of our lives, once we let him.

We also have to be ever so careful about sweet sounding nonsense because as I have repeatedly intimated, Scripture and the media seldom see eye to eye and the media has a way of clothing ludicrous ideology with what seems sensible or even practical.

"When you love someone
And you love them with your heart
And it doesn't disappear if you're apart

When you love someone
And you've done all you can do
When you set them free
And if that love is true
When you love someone
It will all come back to you"

Anita Baker and James Ingram (1996)

This song was formerly a favorite of mine and echoes the sentiments that I held to, and as such made it difficult for me to let go of those feelings that were harmful in my view of how relationships worked. In reality, love is not an uncontrollable emotion, but a conscious decision - we choose to love. The idea then that genuine love would *'come back'* to me, held me hostage to a thought that I did not have to move on because I would get what I wanted and believed to be mine. How did this kind of thinking line up with Scripture? It did not. None of this line of thinking can be reinforced by Scripture. In fact, the ideology being broadcast through these lyrics actually conflicts with what is scriptural since they suggest that love is an entity in and of itself, implying that love, not God was in charge of the situation and orchestrating the path my life would take. Am I reading too much into the lyrics of a song that was merely intended to showcase the talent of two proficient singers? Perhaps I overextend the writers' intentions; but it is with such subtleties that individuals are misguided daily. If it were so insignificant then why did I hold so firmly to this line of thought? Allowing ourselves to move beyond our current feelings of disappointment is more difficult when we not only hang on to our hurt, but also to a mindset that does not promote a Godly way of thinking.

The Divorcee

Similarly, persons who parted before the "*death do us part*" portion of their vows actually materialized must deal with singleness. A Scriptural decision concerning divorce and remarriage may seem very controversial in a society that seems to have rather limited qualms about the issue; and though I claim no profound authority on the interpretation of Scripture, I understand that the covenant a man and woman make before God concerning marriage is a highly serious one that is not to be taken lightly. The basis for Jesus' words in Matthew 19:1 "*...what God has joined together let no man put asunder*" or separate, stem from God's initial plan when he created woman, recorded in Genesis 2. Additionally, the Apostle Paul's exposition on the significance of the marital union's reflection of the relationship between Christ and the Church, suggests that the unions between men and women in this regard are to span their lifetimes. Paul outlines some rather explicit instructions in 1 Corinthians 7:10-16 concerning the conditions surrounding departure from a marriage. Instructions which I dare say are not seriously adhered to even by Christians who occasionally opt to leave their marriages for reasons sometimes equally trivial as those of unbelievers.

The Christian individual who believes his/her relationship has got to the point of such a separation must unyieldingly seek God's intervention for him/herself and spouse. An attempt to move on to another relationship will be hampered by the fact that there are spiritual issues that need to be addressed. Unlike commands concerning sexual immorality or even murder, I do not believe some of the restrictions concerning divorce and remarriage are as explicitly outlined in Scripture; and as such interpretations may sometimes vary and in some cases different inferences may be arrived at. What is clear however is that God certainly does not intend for a whimsical take on the institution of marriage. *'Irreconcilable differences'* which feature most often on many divorce applications are a contrast *and* violation of the instructions that Christians are given regarding their conduct in Ephesians 5:19-24. Developing the Fruit of the Spirit should by extension feature prominently in their marriages. When it pertains to divorce, it is paramount that Christians whose goal is to please God undergo much prayer along with extensive counseling before making such a life changing decision.

Should a believer be faced with the unfortunate experience of getting a divorce, then that person must carefully decide how to live the single life. In my experience very few persons have amicable separations; and often when a marriage gets to the point of divorce, the parties openly express bitterness towards each other. Moving on therefore is often difficult since the pain/ hurt that was endured was a far cry from the perfect smiles and beautiful wardrobe of *that* day, and has left scars that seem impossible to heal. It therefore comes as no surprise that it is difficult to take advice from a person who has never walked the aisle. However, God's word is constant and it tells us to forgive[36] regardless of how wronged we feel.

Forgiveness is perhaps one of the singularly most difficult disciplines of the Christian faith. Yet our very salvation is grounded in it. In order to reconcile mankind with God, the innocent Christ opted to take man's sin upon himself. We become Christians when we seek forgiveness for our sins. It only follows then that we should be willing to forgive those who have hurt us. Entering a new phase of

[36] Colossians 3:13; Ephesians 4:32

being single or even entering a new relationship will pose problematic if that individual is still carrying the "baggage" of a failed relationship. When children are involved there is the added dimension of transferring those feelings of bitterness to the offspring.

The flip side is of course if you are reading this book and you know that the dismantling of your marriage was because of your poor judgment. As difficult and seemingly insignificant as an apology might appear, it is your responsibility as a believer to attempt to make amends. Perhaps circumstances will not allow you to physically let the person know that you have discarded blame or admitted guilt, or such an action will result in more harm than good, only you and God can determine that; but moving on will never truly happen until past guilt/ blame is dealt with.

The divorced single must make all the decisions a single person must make with regards to remaining single, dating or remarriage. For though there is experience brought on from having been down this road before, such persons must be careful not to allow previous expectations and experiences to completely govern subsequent relationships. There may also be the likelihood of hastening decisions because of loneliness, the need for physical support or the seeming security a marriage provides. However, all the things previously mentioned with regard to any unmarried individual is applicable to the person whose marriage has been dissolved. He/she enters into a new relationship with the same considerations as the person who has never married. Although of somewhat a different nature, the Apostle Peter's actions following his denial of Christ,[37] is a profound example of how to move on. His recognition of his mistake did not result in a decision to berate himself and wallow in self pity, Instead, his sadness drove him to make adjustments which were later seen in the role he played in the development of the church.

The Widow/Widower

Finally, like every other aspect of m*oving on,* dealing with the loss of a spouse requires prayer and careful preparation before any

[37] Matthew 26:69 - 75

decision is made concerning dating and remarriage. This of course is dependent on an individual's ability to release the hurt and continue to live. Often some persons refuse to remarry or begin dating again out of a fear that they may seem to have forgotten their deceased spouse. Society too has its "rules" on how long the grieving process should last and many are pitied or ridiculed if their neighbors believe they are "taking too long" or have "moved on too quickly" following the loved one's demise. Although Scripture does not specify how long grieving is to last, it does suggest that to spend an inordinate amount of time mourning the loss of a loved one results in that individual stifling his/her emotional growth. David's response to the death of his son in 2 Samuel 12 perfectly highlights that though a believer may be saddened by a loved one's passing, prolonged weeping and mourning does not result in that loved one's return. David's attitude was one that demonstrated a willingness to accept that God in his infinite wisdom had decided to permit the loved one's death.

It is possible too to move on and simultaneously honor the memory of that loved one who has passed. In Jewish culture, families in which a brother died without leaving an heir saw to it that the name of that deceased brother was continued by mandating a living brother/ nearest male relative of the deceased to marry their family member's widow in order for that deceased son's name to be passed on. Western cultural practices are very different from this and therefore to honor the deceased's memory will take a different format. Some choose to name children, buildings, charities et cetera, in honor of that decedent, others may choose to accredit accomplishments/achievements to their loved one's memory. Regardless of the way chosen, moving on certainly will not equate a dismissal of the loved one's previous existence.

I dare not trivialize the hurt of the loss of a spouse, and recognize that grieving and healing must happen. The widow or widower's decision to remarry or begin dating again should not take place until after this process is complete, regardless of what onlookers may believe. The Christian person's decision to "let go" is in my estimation an exclamation of their faith since they recognize God's overall control of their lives and everything that happens in it. Those who profess to believe in Christ and the validity of the Bible should live in anticipation of seeing their loved ones again, once those persons also believed in Christ.[38]

As such persons begin to return to the dating scene however they must be cognizant of the fact that their decisions are to be thought about and carefully weighed. Like the person who has never married or the divorcee, their new romantic relationships need to undergo as much filtering since a previous marriage does not guarantee expertise in the area of dating and marriage.

Regardless of the circumstances which force you to move on, doing so will only be achieved when you are willing to release the mental and emotional baggage associated with a previous relationship. Do not assume however that moving on means jumping into the next available relationship. It may include remaining single even though you have released the hurt that you have had to endure.

---

[38] 1 Thessalonians 4:13 – 17

Key Reminder: 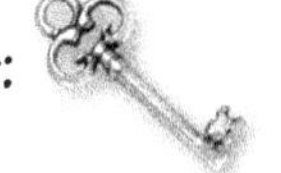

Moving on means releasing the negative vibe of previous relationships

What does this mean for me?

A Date with You, Your Husband/Wife and Some Random Friend... Seriously?

I feel that I must begin this chapter with a disclaimer. I am by no means undermining the genuine interest that some couples have in seeing their single friends dating someone who will complement that friend. Additionally, as I have said, I am well aware that many a romance has been sparked and spurred by the contribution of well meaning friends. On the other hand, what makes some believe that the person whom they think would be "just perfect for their single friend" actually is? I have been on too many blind dates and I blame myself to some extent because I have tried to be polite and respect my friends' interests, opinions and wishes, even to the point of my own discomfort. However I also blame my friends and those like them who attempt to initiate a union not necessarily because they see the compatibility of the individuals but because they believe "it's time," and they rarely see the usefulness/sense of a man/woman remaining single. There is a verse of Scripture that has helped to keep me grounded when society and the persons in my sphere try to suggest that when an individual gets to a certain age he/she must become a spouse and or a parent. Jeremiah 29:11 is a very popular portion of Scripture in Christian circles; and though it primarily spoke to the Israelites in bondage, I contend that it is as applicable to the life of every believer as it was to that of the Israelites those hundreds of years ago. The basic focus of the verse is that God has outlined the path of the believer and that way is one that has been carefully and deliberately plotted. The point then is that regardless of anyone's match making skills, it is the responsibility of that single person to seek God's direction and discover if this "match" lines up with God's plan for his/her life.

First Date

It is still a practice, in some cultures, that the parents of a family arrange the nuptials between their son/daughter and the woman/man they deem most suitable. Most modern cultures however have abolished this practice and as such dating is a natural result. I have read many blogs and articles on the issue of dating and have found it quite interesting how widely the interpretations differ or have evolved. Simplest in its meaning is that a date is a meeting or an appointment, and as such dating would therefore refer to meeting with someone for an appointment. Although some have narrowed the definition to refer to a relationship in which a couple's romantic interests are exclusive to each other, others have suggested that the term applies to those couples that are sexually involved with each other. In recent years the idea of *going out on a date* has been extended to married couples when their excursions are aimed at generating a romantic air. This discussion will however limit the term to those who are unmarried. According to Wikipedia,

> "...*dating is a form of courtship consisting of social activities done by two persons with the aim of each assessing the other's suitability as a partner in an intimate relationship or as a spouse. While the term has several senses, it usually refers to the act of meeting and engaging in some mutually agreed upon social activity in public, together, as a couple*"[39].

That being said, it is important to reflect on the focus of an earlier chapter in which the importance of being true to who you are was highlighted. When knowledge of self and subsequent truthfulness is exhibited, then the process of dating will become less uncertain.

---

[39] http://en.wikipedia.org/wiki/Dating_(activity)

Before That Date

In this high-tech era, match making has evolved from "the nice lady who sits two seats behind you in church trying to set you up with her nephew" to actual dating sites, some professing to be a site for Christian singles to meet. Although I have never visited any such site, neither would I dare to speak against them, the message I have been propagating over these several pages is constant; has the individual truly sought God's opinion? For whether it is an online dating service or a liaising friend, the single person must be ready to act according to God's directive. It takes great effort to hear God's instruction when you have already made up your mind as to what you want. But it is at those times that we are most vulnerable and prone to making mistakes that may ruin our lives completely or take us down paths that could have been avoided.

Of all the persons who seemed least likely to err in this regard was the great King Solomon, deemed to have been the wisest man who ever lived. However when he took wives from among the peoples God had instructed

Israel not to, it resulted in his heart being momentarily turned away from God. The Book of Ecclesiastes expounds King Solomon's discovery that wives, wealth or wisdom would not add meaning and significance to life. After all his searching and despite failures, he concluded rather succinctly that humans ought to *"Fear God and keep his commandments, for this is the whole duty of man"*[40]. It is in fact a relationship with the Creator and God of the Universe that will fill the voids that humans have.

I love my friends who are married and would not be so presumptuous as to suggest that they do not have my best interest at heart. It is however important to accept that if you are married, your single friend(s) may not be enthused about double dating with you and your spouse and that person you are currently trying to fix him/her up with. Unless of course your single friend is comfortable with such match making and has given you the go ahead, stop trying to play cupid. It is instinctive in some of our natures to fix what we think is wrong in

[40] Ecclesiastes 12:13 (KJV)

somebody else's life; and because society often views singleness with that "something's wrong" attitude, persons go to great lengths to try to help the single person in that regard. It is faulty to see your life (if you are single) as being broken solely because of your singleness. Undoubtedly if there are character flaws or other issues to address, then such things must be repaired; but do not, under any circumstances, accept the notion that your singleness is your flaw.

Similarly, there are some persons whom God has given the grace to remain single. Who are we to try and fix that?[41] As the Apostle Paul noted, it is important, if your intention is to become a faithful steward in God's kingdom, to be honest with yourself and to act accordingly[42]. One of the gravest injustices to Christendom is those who outwardly declare a life of celibacy and purity in order to serve Christ yet clandestinely feed their sexual lusts. It not only brings the ministry of God in disrepute, but causes those who are genuine in their

[41] St. Matthew 19:12

[42] I Corinthians 7:8-9

commitments to be disbelieved, mistrusted or even discouraged.

I almost feel as though I am repeating myself; but can it really be said enough? Any person desiring to serve Christ must first get over him/herself. I credit Rick Warren's *Purpose Driven Life®* for helping in revolutionizing my view of life. When we start viewing our lives from the vantage point that our existence goes beyond our current and even future situations, then decision making becomes less about what we think we will get out of it and more about what purpose God has for our lives in particular situations. *"It's not about you. The purpose of your life is far greater than your own personal fulfillment, your peace of mind, or even your happiness"*[43]. Talk about humbling? This statement captures that completely. I have heard friends share that they were offended when they read it. "How could my life not be about me?" they ask. But Warren is merely reiterating what the Word of God already said as he also quotes from the Book of Colossians 1:16

[43] *Purpose Driven Life©,* Rick Warren, Zondervan 2002, p.17

"For by him all things were created...all things were created by him and for him."

Columbia Pictures' 2006 film production of an aspect of multi-millionaire stock broker Chris Gardner's life in *The Pursuit of Happyness,* would typically be referred to as a tear jerker, since audiences get to see actor Will Smith dramatize the real life struggle of a man who truly epitomized what Thomas Edison referred to when he said "there is no substitute for hard work". Kudos to Chris Gardner for the sheer grit he exhibited in order to achieve his financial success. Despite his success however, it is my earnest hope that his pursuit for true happiness was not primarily financial for though he garnered much materially, if therein lies the apex of his quest, then his pursuit and that of countless others is far from over. I found the movie to be a very motivational one; but from the viewpoint of the life of a born again believer in Jesus Christ it was just that, a movie. Our pursuit must surpass material gain; and for the purposes of our current discussion, relational or emotional gain. The pursuit of the persons who have devoted themselves to Christ must be to achieve lives in which God is glorified. Dating merely for the sake of quelling a feeling of loneliness is by far one of the most unproductive activities I have carried out in my life. Now, when I refuse a friend's attempts to pair me with one of their *available* friends, I do so not because of feelings of superiority, but because I recognize the futility of dating *just because* I am single.

I stand corrected if my conclusions are incorrect, but there is no "love at first sight" magical feeling that sustains a relationship. In fact, I have come to understand that relationships that stand the tests of time and disappointment do so only because the individuals have made a conscious decision to hold fast to their commitments to each other. In their *Love at Last Sight* © Kerry and Chris Shook delve deeply into ways we can identify the genuineness of our love. Although the Shooks' study addresses relationships in general, romantic relationships require the same intentionality. The crux of their discussion is *"the best relationships – the ones that are long lasting and withstand the test of time – require dedication, trust and commitment"*[44]. In the lives of believers, it is my conviction that there is added strength accorded to us when we rely on Christ's influence in our relationships.

The underlining point is that very rarely do single individuals achieve much satisfaction from attending a barrage of dates. Those who are convinced that they have been called to a life of singleness often feel pressured and frustrated when their friends constantly attempt to get them to participate in dates, since such actions are actually counterproductive. Frustration can also materialize for those who, although they may not be convinced of God's decision for them to lead a life of singleness, they are tired of the numerous unfruitful, even unwise attempts they have made while attempting to not disappoint their friends.

To the married I admonish you to talk to your single friends about dating if you are trying to match them with another. As your friendship allows you to talk about any other activity in your life, be bold enough to discover if your

---

[44] Love at Last Sight©, Waterbrook Press, 2010

actions are in fact being deemed helpful. If you do not know the person well enough, or are uncomfortable with addressing this topic, then perhaps you have no business in this area of your friend's life. Being single is not an illness and you should not attempt to connect your friend with another merely because he or she is single. You should know your friend well enough to be able to make worthwhile suggestions to them concerning possible dates *if they are so inclined.* To the single, my advice comes from my own experiences. Do not date frivolously to please your friends. Instead, seek to pursue God with all your heart. Those who are busily doing what God would have them to do will be led as God's people usually are, to having the necessary things *"added"*[45]. I am in no way dismissing the recommendations that are sometimes given; but I believe that many disappointments can be avoided when our approach is more deliberately structured. As Andy Stanley so profoundly expresses it, *"Direction–not intentions, hopes, dreams, prayers, beliefs, intellect, or*

[45] Matthew 6:23

education–determines destination."[46] If there is a particular goal you wish to achieve in your life, in this case your marital future, then the direction of that life must be strategically planned.

[46] *The Principle of the Path*, Andy Stanley, Thomas Nelson 2009

Key Reminder:

Having random dates is not the most prudent way to deal with singleness

What does this mean for me?

6

Propose Already!

If my own experience has been occasionally annoying because people keep asking me when I intend to get married, I know then that my single friends who have been dating specific individuals for a while have it even more difficult than I do. For not only must they deal with their own emotions regarding their next step; but they must also deal with the *prying* well wishers who are almost insistent that a date be named for the 'big day'. This practice is most common among church people, many of whom are this way because they question the ability of the persons to maintain sexual purity if they are dating over an extended period. If God has led you to marriage then you must be certain you have been hearing from Him instead of being influenced by the catalogues that show the most gorgeous dresses, the sparkle of that absolutely exquisite ring, the glamour of the wedding day itself and not the marriage, or the seeming respect accorded to those who are married. Undoubtedly, women face the brunt of social pressure regarding this issue of marriage; but men also endure the strain of being *forced* as it were to, to propose.

The long relationship between Britain's Duke and Duchess of Cambridge was one that received extensive scrutiny from the media all around the world. Naturally because of the Prince's popularity their relationship faced more criticisms than that of the average couple. British tabloids went as far to refer to the Duchess as "Waitey Katey" simply because the media had presumed that having been in a relationship with the prince for so long without a marriage proposal, she was simply waiting around for him. To some extent I admire the decision of the Duke and Duchess, and those who think and act as they did simply because they believed they needed to clarify things for themselves prior to entering into a commitment that, despite secular opinion, is still a sacred institution. Living together prior to marriage is however against what God has stipulated and this is where I believe the royal couple erred.

I already referred to the importance of being true to self; and the façade that is often removed only *after* the "I dos" is something couples must seek to make a greater effort at removing altogether. Undoubtedly people's opinions and goals change and normal human beings have varying opinions, it is therefore understandable that unforeseen disagreements will materialize after marriage; however at what point in our lives do we compromise? Perhaps I am being idealistic, but do believers not have the advantage of a superior power helping them in this aspect of their lives? Or is it that they are not tapping into this resource? Despite the adjustments that our world has made in redefining marriage, it is nevertheless an institution created by God to reflect the union between the church and himself. Why are we then so often cavalier in our view of marriage and what it reflects? Perhaps we have got to the stage where we no longer see marriage in this light and as such feel free to propose and accept proposals according to our whims and fancies. Too often it is the questioning glances, whispers or outright probing of close friends and even mere acquaintances that become the driving force behind many people's decision to finally *"tie the knot"*.

Is there a time limit on dating or an engagement? Certainly God has called Christian people to live a particular life and part of that life requires that we maintain sexual purity; and as cited earlier, the Apostle Paul addressed this issue in I Corinthians when he admonished dating believers on the actions they should take if the physical passion of their relationship prevented them from maintaining the aforementioned purity. Sexual desires are God-given, and as such natural, therefore please do not dismiss my statements as judgments against them. Such desires however, cannot be the *sole* reason for marriage if you are attempting to live a life for Christ. The onus is then on us to examine what it is we hope to achieve for Christ in this life and use that as the basis or starting point for all other decisions that we make.

I do… Because

It requires great conviction on the part of both parties to neither succumb to the social pressure of marrying for appearances' sake, or to the physical pressure of gratifying their physical desires before they are ready to commit to all the requirements of a marriage. If you have ever had to make this decision I do not envy you at all. I know I would rather be single than marry merely for sexual gratification. The introduction outlined what I believe are often erroneous reasons some persons choose to get married; and if you are at this stage of your life I implore you to carefully ensure that your hand is not being forced by a circumstance which cannot sustain your union once that circumstance has been altered.

Marriage has become so trivialized in Western Culture that many people, both Christian and non-Christian alike, sometimes question "*Why bother?*" The devil has successfully fooled many into believing that marriage is defined by the couple; and once a prenuptial agreement has been signed or persons "fall out of love with each other", then each party can start life "afresh" when the dissolution of the marriage has been recognized by the courts (sometimes even before). From the beginning of man's existence however, God obviously had a bigger purpose in creating the union between man and woman[47]. When God made woman, he did so to meet a need that He created in man as he described man's being alone as "unsuitable"[48]. In giving man and woman the ability to procreate, then the development of community is the natural result. Scripture does not suggest however that *all* men and *all* women are to be married or God would not have directed Paul to speak as he did in Corinthians. On the other hand, Scripture does direct us to seek God's kingdom first and God will allow all other things to fall into place. As one's success in living life as a single person requires dependence on God, so too a couple's marital life depends on God's sustenance and direction.

A previous chapter delved into what the single believer should do in order to circumvent the temptation of sexual sin; but even if a couple does yield to the temptation of becoming

[47] Genesis 2:24; Matthew 19:5-6

[48] Genesis 2:18 (NIV)

sexually active before they are married and the woman becomes pregnant, marrying because of this situation is not a good idea either. Unlike the Apostle Paul I do not claim to be an oracle of God, however I believe there are some things that God has allowed me to recognize and these are the bases for this line of argument. Pregnancy is not a sin! It is the sexual act between the unmarried that is. Therefore marrying someone *because of* a pregnancy in no way corrects the sexual sin though society and even church would sometimes like to suggest that it does. I would never suggest to a friend that he or she marry solely for those reasons, because what happens to the relationship after the child is born, or if the fetus dies? Can a union built solely on the pressure created by a pregnancy be sustained throughout a lifetime of marriage? Getting married to solve a problem, which is what a pregnancy in this case becomes equivalent to, will undoubtedly create many new ones.

Many of us have heard stories of both men and women who feel or have felt trapped in a marriage that only occurred because of a pregnancy. It is arguable that such a marriage can yield favorable results by creating emotional stability for the child when both parents commit to each other in order to rear the child together, and that child is not forced to deal with the uncertainties that sometimes arise when parents have separate homes. Additionally, there is some measure of security when incomes are pooled for a common purpose. The reverse however is obviously true. A child can as easily be affected if his parents are feuding. "Shot gun" marriages as they are colloquially referred, are as dangerous as they sound. Statistics do prove that such marriages have a higher failure rate than many others. Certainly there have been successful unions of this sort, and there are numerous other reasons marriages have failed. But is it wise to make or accept a proposal if the only reason is a pregnancy? Marriage has so much more to offer. Do not compound the mistake of sexual impropriety by making a decision that, though revocable by law, carries with it emotionally, physically and sometimes financially draining repercussions.

Yet another question I know that a few seriously dating singles must deal with is the question of "when?" *"When is the right time for us to go to the marriage stage of our relationship?"* They must ask themselves.

"Should we go to that stage?" "What are the factors/ reasons preventing us from or pointing us to a marital move?" Like every other important aspect of life, such decisions should be seriously prayed and thought out before actions are taken. What should never influence the move however, is the desire to maintain an image. Our generation of two–minute meals, microwave pop-corn, instant oats and instant gratification, has led us to live lives in which we are constantly rushing, hurriedly making decisions, the repercussions of which are unfortunately far reaching and even damning. Unlike the disciples of Acts whom Jesus told to "*wait for the Promise of the Father*"[49] we have become accustomed to having everything immediately that we refuse to wait on God's directives.

[49] Acts 1:4 KJV

Key Reminder:

Getting married '*just because*' is not the best idea for the dating single

What does this mean for me?

God's Best

My high school was about twenty miles from where I lived, and public transportation for school kids in the early 90s was not a favorable experience for those of us in the rural parts of Jamaica. The buses were few; and since children paid half the portion of fare adults did, we were forced by the bus operators at the terminal to wait until all the seats were filled before we were allowed to jostle for standing space for our 1½ hours bus ride. By the time I was a senior however I had learnt that most times if I waited long enough for the rush to pass, my journey home was not as hectic and uncomfortable. While I waited I would sometimes complete assignments at the library, participate in after school programs I would perhaps have otherwise ignored, or just hang out with my friends (since there was no Facebook or instant messaging, and telephone conversations for the average person were limited to three way calls via land lines). As waiting did not guarantee my bus rides would be stress free, I am not trying to suggest that marrying later in life will automatically mean a better deal, I am simply suggesting that rushing may not result in our expectations being met. We miss out on getting a better experience because we are too preoccupied with just falling within what we perceive the *norm* to be. Because of this, some enter their marriages without first developing some necessary attributes that would better contribute to their marriages' success.

Undoubtedly there are many men and women who would have made better spouses if they had better prepared themselves for marriage. For some, preparation would have meant a delay in their decision, for others it would mean that their goals or expectations of marriage would have been less on what they desired and more about what they recognized God's plan to be.

Scripture is abundantly clear that God created marriage for the purposes of companionship, procreation and the reflection of the divine union between Christ and the Church (Christians)[50]. It also makes it clear that not all individuals are to be married, as cited in the portions quoted from 1 Corinthians 7. Of those who marry, socialization and other circumstances will result in the union of some immediately out of their teens; still others will marry much later in life. The need to therefore understand how to live a life that reflects a commitment to Christ while unmarried is what this book has attempted to explore. What ought Christian men and women to do while single? Whether this singleness is a lifelong one or merely until… Their lives are to be spent developing their characters as loving, joyful, peaceful, patient, kind, good and faithful[51] individuals. By first developing the Fruit of the Spirit spoken about by the Apostle Paul in

[50] Genesis 2:18; 1:28; Ephesians 5:23 - 32
[51] Galatians 5:22

Galatians, they would be happier and more productive persons who have not confined themselves to an idea that marriage is the only determinant for personal development and change.

The entire concept of achieving God's best stems from a willingness to seek His direction and wait on His answer before making any moves. Determining God's directives to certain specific steps the Christian will make will be dependent on that individual's communication with God. People who share my opinion on the issue in relation to marriage are often called *picky, snobbish, foolish* even *hyper spiritual*. Yet if they do indeed share my line of thought they are not looking for Mr/Miss Perfect, but Mr/Miss Perfect for *me*. I use the expression *looking for* rather loosely here because persons of this mindset do not go through each day pining away with the hope of 'finding' a suitable mate, but recognize that though one can be happy in a marriage, it is not the marriage that will make you happy. The expression "looking for" thus speaks to those who are open to the idea that God has included marriage as a part of His plan for their lives. The recurring idea being presented is that God's best cannot be acquired if either your motives or focus is wrong; and sometimes God's best will mean remaining single.

God's so Particular

The good thing about the God we serve is that He knows and understands us in a way that we do not even understand ourselves. He will never give us more than we are able to bear[52], and this applies to every aspect of our lives. If God has called you to a life of singleness do not let the pressure and expectations of those around you dictate that you do anything else. Likewise, if for whatever reason you are currently single and not dating anyone, do not assume that your state is tantamount to boredom and misery. If you are single, meaning unmarried, yet in a committed relationship, do not allow any of the 'Not to' reasons I mentioned in the introduction, force you to make a decision neither you nor your significant other is fully committed to making. Remember that God's purposes for your life extend beyond a marriage. Though God desires that we have some comfort in our

[52] 1Cointhians 10:13

lives, He has an ultimate plan that does not involve our focus to be solely earth centered.

Additionally, God never contradicts himself. His best therefore can never be contrary to his Scriptural specifications and this is where so many Christians, decade after decade have failed. We get so caught up in wanting some temporal things that we lose sight of our eternal purpose. I am yet to meet that Christian person who opted to find his/ her mate outside of God's stipulations and has not in some way regretted that move. There is often at this time a misuse of prayer. Misuse because we are sometimes guilty of praying for direction on an issue that God has explicitly ruled against. The prayer instead should be one for divine strength to accept what in and of ourselves we do not wish to because our emotions are running contrary to what God has instructed. On the other hand, the unfortunate reality is a man/woman's profession to know the Lord does not guarantee blissful days and a *happily ever after* union either. Situations are nevertheless compounded when one party is not of a similar spiritual persuasion. It is very easy to become blind-sided by the charm of the person one is romantically interested in, however if that person does not share your faith in Jesus Christ, more often than not, the believer's heart is turned away from God as was the case of so many of Israel's kings when they compromised God's commands regarding marriage to 'foreign women' or permitting idolatrous peoples to live near to them and serve their gods.

Among the most saddening stories of Biblical history is that of Samson's rise and fall. Although Samson's death resulted in the destruction of thousands of Philistines, his life demonstrated the results of a life only partially committed to God's will. I would implore you to invest the time to read through the chapters of Judges (Chapters 13 – 16) that speak of Samson's life and death. Before Samson was born, God had outlined a task for his life[53]. Although God used Samson's weakness for foreign women, as he had done with Pharaoh's pride[54], to complete his ultimate purpose - begin the Israelites' rescue from God's enemies, Samson did not experience the complete satisfaction of God's call on his life because he opted to do some things his way. It is difficult

---

[53] Judges 13:5

[54] Exodus 9 & 10

when we are in the moment to realize and act upon what we know is best when our desires go contrary to God's wishes. However if we do not lose sight of God's overall picture and purpose then our results will be great.

I recall when I was seventeen years old and my father told me that I should ensure that my date for the annual summer camp banquet knew the Lord. I thought his instructions were rather odd since it was only a three hour dinner. I was particularly annoyed because that year I had intended to attend the banquet with a young man whom I was attracted to. I knew his feelings were similar and so we had arranged to go to the banquet with each other long before the camp had even started, and then my father threw this curve ball at me. My father and I have never talked about that summer. Perhaps it was the Spirit of God that revealed the need for him to say this, since prior to (or following) that year he had never given me dating advice though I had been attending that summer camp since I had been nine years old and continued to attend way into my 20s. Perhaps he knew of my intentions or maybe he felt I was at the age where he needed to closely monitor my dealings with persons of the opposite sex. Whatever the reason, his instructions resulted in me being dateless at that banquet as Ephesians 6: 1 - 3 had for years been drilled into my psyche and I thought it was essential to respect the wishes of my parents. I obeyed with a very heavy heart and had been too disappointed to accept the proposals of any other young man during that week.

Gary Williams, my youth pastor during my teen years, also often said that "every date was a potential mate" as he too warned us against dating individuals who did not know the Lord. Unfortunately, those words of wisdom have only truly made sense to me now while as an adult I am seeking to become more seriously committed to my relationship with Christ. Although I have not always followed my father's instructions as I did that summer, I completely see the merit of them; and I have repeatedly regretted any decision to act contrary. It has taken me a while, but I thank God I have finally put into practice what His Word has been guiding. As a teen I disagreed with my father's view and thought it nonsensical; but it was foolhardy to think that since I did not intend to marry the persons I dated who did not know the Lord, there was no harm in dating them. *No harm no foul* right? Wrong. The concept of unequal yoking[55] is multi-faceted I have learnt; it extends to marriages, business partners, best friends, dates and the list goes on. Now, when I meet a 'decent' or 'Christian minded' nonbeliever, I do not go on a date to be polite, or date with the intention to eventually 'win him over'. The latter is a particular lie Christians, myself included, have frequently told themselves. A desire to *convert* an individual solely for the purposes of making that person appropriate for you to date and perhaps later marry, is not only selfish but runs the risk of failure since that individual may temporarily follow the routine of Christianity in order to please you. Certainly persons genuinely make professions of faith in Christ but that does not negate the believer's responsibility to obey what God has said. Until I arrived at the place where I realized God's best could only be achieved once the preparatory work of obedience to Him had been done, it did not appear to me that singleness and happiness could be used in the same sentence.

---

[55] 2 Corinthians 6:14-17

Regardless of what our end motives are, God does not require our assistance and His best is better achieved without our contributions. The attempts to help Him out or prod Him along has for generations resulted in less than satisfactory results. King Saul's decision in 1 Samuel 13:1 – 14 resulted in his kingdom over Israel being curtailed when he opted to undertake tasks that God had specifically outlined for someone else. Likewise Abraham and Sarah's decision to 'help' God fulfill the promise of the creation of the nation of Israel, by turning to Hagar[56], continues to wreak havoc in the Middle East as the descendants of Ishmael and Isaac are at constant odds with each other. The point is God prefers that His instructions be followed regardless of how inconvenient they appear or how well meaning our motives may be[57]
.

I have heard accounts of Christians who, from as early as their teen years, knew that singleness is what they believed they had been called to as they serve Christ. Knowing God's plan in this regard however is immaterial to me

---

[56] Genesis 15-17

[57] 1 Samuel 15;22

since my primary focus has been altered. I stated in the opening that I know that at this time I am not prepared to be married since other than for sexual gratification or the glamour of being gorgeously dressed and being the center of attention for a day, I cannot think of a reason I would want to be married or the usefulness it would serve in my current life. We have touched on the reasons these sole desires are unsuitable for a marriage to thrive as God intends. My wholehearted wish is that Christian singles will embrace the fact that our main desires are to be centered on living lives that please and glorify God first. As this is done, the amazing result is that He will allow our other desires (that will by extension stem from an understanding of His will for our lives) to be materialized. A twice married, once divorced friend of mine told me that it is better to remain single than be in a bad marriage. Though he often tries not to dwell on his past mistakes, he is adamant that the failure of his first marriage hinged on the fact that he married for what he terms the 'wrong' reasons, and as a direct result he married the 'wrong' person.

Is it possible for two believers, who intend to marry each other, to cheat themselves of acquiring God's best? By all means yes. Scripture does specifically speak to an incompatibility between light and darkness in reference to the union of believers and unbelievers; however because of personality differences along with differences in life goals and value systems, a marital union even between believers can face discord if the individuals are not on the same page with regard to these belief systems. Although this situation is more easily corrected since you will be looking to the same source, God, for guidance. It is important to nevertheless be aware of whatever beliefs and goals your *intended* might possess. If God's call on your life is different from his/hers, then a union between you both will undoubtedly be strained.

The right or wrong choice for believers is going to be ascertained by those persons' decisions to put themselves in the position to acquire the best that God has for them; and God's best is only going to be gained by following God's instructions. In Episode 215 of the 2009 season of *Love Marriage and Stinking Thinking*, Mark Gungor reiterates the fact that acquiring God's best can only occur when we are being obedient to Him instead of focusing on what we believe is best for us:

> *"...you can't live by your feelings, if you live by your feelings you will be a disaster, that's why we have the Bible... this is our point of reference...You can't trust your feelings... By following God's principles you judge those principles against your feelings and then make the right choices"*

Coupled with following God's instructions in His Word to us, a call to prayer and spiritual living must not be taken lightly. If we intend to gain the best that God has to offer then there is a necessity to be in tune with His directives and the path that He would have us to chart in our daily lives. Following those instructions will often prove difficult, but it is impossible to argue contrary to the fact that the benefits exceed the tiresomeness.

Don't cheat yourself!

What does this mean for me?

What Now?

Every time I read a directional book of any kind my favorite chapter is the one that outlines what the next suggested move is. Throughout the previous chapters, I have attempted to discuss some essentials that I believe every single person must consider. This chapter then aims at summarizing some specific steps that must be taken as you continue/ begin to live lives that are meaningful declarations of the God you claim to serve. Being single is not solely being unmarried, because if you profess to know the Lord it also means there are some societal 'norms' that you will be required to abstain from because of this commitment. Singleness almost then becomes warfare and there is a tug-of-war between what you know you must do and what you sometimes desire to do. There is an important question that only the individual can answer: *by whose standards am I living?* The standards by which you live are a result of who you allow to call the shots in your life. If you are taking your cues from the latest or most popular bachelor/ bachelorette reality series, or from the crooning of your favorite singer, then your decision making will be skewed and happiness will continue to be elusive, for though we live in this world, Scripture advises that we cannot be governed by it since the world's principles will more often than not conflict with God's.[58]

As a believer, it is God's Word that ought to determine the standards by which you live. Certainly it is often difficult, but like every other worthwhile thing, it will only be achieved

[58] 1 John 2:15 - 17

through self sacrifice. Self denial is hard and is even viewed as foolish or impossible, yet it is with this tar that the Christian path has been paved.[59] Denial of certain physical and material desires because our focus must extend beyond our present existence, is an attribute not easily acquired but not at all impossible. If however you are not a believer in Jesus Christ, then the first thing I beg you to do is ask God's forgiveness for your sin. Contrary to secular belief, it is not profitable to ask Him to sort out the relationship aspect of your life if you have cordoned off everywhere else.[60] When He controls your heart then all other steps become relevant for application.

I have already suggested that Christian women seem to have the hardest time dealing with being single for a number of reasons. Among these is the seeming time constraint on reproduction (although Sarah and Elizabeth would perhaps argue differently[61]) and suitable mates in church seem somewhat elusive.

[59] Luke 9:23
[60] Psalm 66:18
[61] Genesis 18:10- 11;21:2; Luke 1:36-37

Ironically not many men seem to be desirous of faithfully serving God, contrasting it seems with the obvious role God intended for them. In my experience, Caribbean women in particular have had grave difficulty because most Caribbean churches are female dominated. As a result, the temptation to go out and *find one to bring in*, has always been a hurdle for the Christian women in many churches. I will hasten to warn women however that the book of Proverbs highlights that *"He who finds a wife finds what is good"*[62], suggesting therefore that it is not the woman's responsibility to go in search of a mate. Perhaps too when women are busy doing the things that will make them attractive individuals (and of course I refer to things beyond the superficial such as hair and makeup) then those who are indeed desirous of becoming wives will be discovered by the persons who not only please God, but will please them as well.

The Bible repeatedly reinforces the principles God has stipulated. When, upon Abraham's commission, Abraham's chief servant went in search of a wife for Isaac,

[62] Proverbs 18:22 (NIV)

Genesis 24 reveals a beautiful account of the servant's faith and dependence upon God's divine intervention in the selection of a spouse for his master's son. What is more striking is the fact that it was in carrying out her duties that Rebekah demonstrated her suitability to become Isaac's wife. Similarly, Ruth, in the book of Ruth, won Boaz's favor through her diligence in helping her aged mother-in-law. Her motives did not lie in finding a spouse. In fact, despite Naomi's warning that she remain in Moab where it was more likely for her to be able to remarry, Ruth decided to commit herself to a woman whom in a real sense she was no longer bound to since her husband Mahlon, Naomi's son, was now dead; yet she committed to serving Naomi's God and traveling with Naomi to Judah. After dutifully serving and being obedient to her mother-in-law's instructions, Ruth was able to marry a thoughtful and wealthy man. Esther likewise, in the book titled same, followed the instructions of her uncle, Mordecai, and later became Queen even after she somewhat plainly presented herself before King Xerxes.[63] Because of her faith in God she garnered the king's favor

[63] Esther 2: 13, 15

and was instrumental in saving the lives of the Jewish people in the region of Persia. In each case the woman fulfilled her duties and allowed God to orchestrate His plans in her life. When individuals zone in on God's picture, then the scenes of their lives fall into place and make sense.

When we work off our own initiative, though some success may be achieved we rob ourselves of God's ultimate blessing. Moses' frustration because of his situation in Numbers 20, prompted him to strike the rock in anger when God had instructed him to speak to the rock. Though the rock emitted water, God punished Moses by disallowing him to enter the land of Canaan. God is serious about His people's obedience; and though we are fortunate to live in an era in which punishment is not as immediate as it had been in the past, since we live in the time of God's grace instead of the time of the law[64], it does not negate our responsibility to adhere His wishes because we still must answer to Him for the lives we live. If we are spirit-filled every aspect of our lives

64 Romans 6:14

will be touched; and although this book is particularly focused on the life of the single man or woman, I think it is important to highlight that the principal of permitting God's complete reign can be applied to every facet of our lives.[65]

Ask yourself if you have cheated yourself of receiving God's best by the selections you have made in the dates you have chosen? Use God's Word to help you negotiate His directives for your life. The individual who seeks to live a life that is sold out to Christ must begin by applying God's principles to that life. Why is something that sounds so simple so difficult to perform? Through the Apostle Paul, Scripture warns that we fight a spiritual battle,[66] one that cannot be fought by sheer will power. God has however given us the wherewithal to battle those unseen forces that will come and oppose us; and this means our weapons must therefore be spiritual.[67]

---

[65] Matthew 6:33

[66] 2 Corinthians 10:4

[67] Ephesians 6: 11 -18

Key Reminder:

Your next move involves obedience to God

What does this mean for me?

FAQs

Frequently Asked Questions

Here I try to broach some of the most popular concerns in relation to the issue of singleness and marriage. Like the content of the rest of this book, the answers are based on a Biblical approach. Naturally not all responses will feel easy, but the ones that are in obedience to God's directives do yield the best result.

1. Really, what's taking God so long?

Finite man measures everything in seconds, minutes, hours, days, weeks, you get the picture; but Scripture tells us that a thousand years to God are like one day and vice versa [68]. In order to strike the balance between the seeming time constraints we have and the infinity of God's timing, we have to remember and

[68] 2 Peter 3:8

acknowledge that the life yielded to Him is perfectly planned and that nothing is by happenstance. Instead of questioning God's seeming delay why not work on improving one's character? If marriage is something that means so much, discover what aspects of your life upon improvement would make you a better husband or wife[69].

2. ***What's my next move if I've already messed up in the area of marriage?***

One thing about God that bowls me over is His willingness to forgive us even after we have gone our own way. God is just, and so there will be consequences that we may have to deal with, but He never turns His back on the truly penitent. "Messing up" has various degrees and therefore your actions will be dependent on what it is. For example if you have become frustrated in a marriage, that had you been

---

[69]Ephesians 5:; 22-29; Proverbs 31:10-30

better informed or had followed God's leading you would not have gone into, then you need to pray for God's intervention. It may also be necessary to speak to that spouse about seeking a marriage counselor as soon as possible. Unless of course your life is being threatened, it is your duty as a believer to make every effort to make it work.

Old Testament Scripture repeatedly tells that despite numerous warnings, God's people, the Israelites, frequently strayed. God was however waiting in the wings each time they sought His forgiveness. Similarly, Jesus had predicted the Apostle Peter's denial of Him, yet when Peter later repented he was forgiven. Jesus waits to forgive the truly penitent and will even strengthen us as we deal with the repercussions of poor decisions.

3. Are Singles' Ministries a worthwhile venture in churches?

In my experience very few churches are sensitive enough to the needs of its single parishioners. Most sermons are targeted at the married; and singles often have to "play it by air" or do their own studies. Either that or some instructions are stapled to the tail end of a sermon on marriage telling singles what to do until they get married, as though marriage was but a year away. Yet not enough time is spent delving into how adults who may never marry or who may spend ten to fifteen or more years single are to faithfully serve Christ during the years of singleness. Certainly it is necessary to invest in the development of this group of persons in any church. Singles' ministries like every other ministry in the church should be tailored to suit the needs of the Christian single from a spiritual and social point of view. Secular media is too often left to mold the views of single persons and that accounts for much of the struggles faced in this aspect of our lives.

Churches do need singles' ministries, especially when they have a fairly large group of unmarried persons.

For smaller congregations where there are not enough persons available to facilitate the formation of a formal group, more exhortation from the pulpit should become commonplace. While there may not be a separate ministry especially for singles in small congregations, social activities geared towards meeting their social needs should nevertheless be organized. It is my belief that large numbers often stray away from the church during their young adult single lives, only to return when they are married and “settled”. This is not an excuse but it is worthwhile to consider that many act in this way because there are not enough support groups within the church i.e groups of persons who can help chart the lives of such persons who are seeking friendship and fun, outside of a weekly church service.

This is a reality that must be faced and tackled within the church. Certainly it is not the programs that will determine an individual’s decision to be faithful in service to the Lord, but it is definite that everyone needs encouragement or the Apostle Paul would not have needed to admonish the older women to teach the younger women[70]; nor would James have instructed that we pray for each other[71] and show concern for each other's weaknesses and needs[72].

4. *What if the person I'm dating is "God-minded" but hasn't made an "official" commitment to Christ?*

I've met some non-Christians who seemingly have better attitudes and sometimes principles than some who profess to have experienced salvation. *"God-mindedness"* is however not enough to determine if that person is right for the Christian person. An awareness of God is something that even Satan and his demons have[73] which signals that

---

[70] Titus 2:4-5

[71] James 5:16

[72] James 5:19

[73] James 2:19

awareness is not enough. Why has that person opted not to commit him/herself to Christ? God has said 'no' and so should you. Allow God to give you his best.

5. Is sexual abstinence during singleness a practical reality?

Scripture says it is and I'll piggy back on that. If God did not intend for us to accomplish something he never would have asked us to do it. Sexual temptation, like every other can be fought by reliance on God's strength[74]. It seems initially difficult because we are more often than not sidetracked by popular secular values; but if we walk after/ follow the Spirit we will not fulfill fleshly lusts[75]. The ability to practically embrace abstinence will not materialize before a recognition that

[74] 1 Corinthians 10:13

[75] Galatians 5:16-17

temptation in this area is real and requires divine intervention if it is to be dealt with.

6. ***How does one move on after you think you've met the love of your life and that relationship is broken?***

Scripture does point to the fact that even the unpleasant experiences have a God-ordained purpose. It's never easy to accept these difficult circumstances, and the first human reaction is to ask God "why me?" Especially if we've done all the right things as far as we know it, we begin to question whether this disappointment is deserved. If your circumstance does not reflect your expectations, believe that God, though he cares about your needs, has a purpose that He desires to achieve in your life[76] despite your negative experience. If you're suddenly single because of a break up or

[76] John 9:3

death, allow yourself to heal from that relationship's end, but recognize that hanging on renders you unhappy *and* ineffective in God's army.

7. ***Even Church people give me a hard time because I am single, how do I get them off my back?***

Equalizing singleness with some type of failure or incompleteness is a misconception that seems to bridge a gap between the church and the world. Both groups tend to attach an air of accomplishment to marriage that is both misleading and unfair to those who are not married. We must not settle for a relationship, especially a marital one, merely to be less conspicuous. Instead when it comes up, adopt the attitude that you are in no rush and are waiting on God to confirm a relationship (He actually does that). If the persons are not in your inner circle and are being more inquisitive than helpful, dismiss them politely with a smile and remember that even if you are in a relationship, people will find something to *give advice* about. If God has confirmed it to you that marriage is not a part of His purpose for you, say it. Your genuine friends will get the picture. You don't really need to care what the others think.

8. How does one deal with the water cooler talk that I've moved on too quickly following my spouse's death?

No one but the individual in the situation can truly gauge how grief is handled, and as such no one but the individual can decide when to move on. As long as the decision to remarry or begin dating again is not a method of stifling grief then go for it. Merely numbing the pain can have very negative repercussions for both the person in grief and the unlucky man or woman being used as a buffer, so grief counseling is always recommended. That new date or spouse must be given a fair chance; therefore such a decision should never be taken lightly, and should be approached with much prayer and keen directives from God. Like everything else, those within your inner circle of friends will be privy to your progress and as such will not be greatly alarmed by your moves. The opinions of the others, as I said before, are irrelevant.

9. ***Seeing someone for a few hours and days each week is entirely different from seeing them every day after you've married them. Don't common law unions prior to marriage have a proven effectiveness?***

How well can one person truly know another? Admittedly many spouses are rudely awakened by some less than favorable habits that were concealed during the dating stage of the relationship but revealed once the couple began to live with each other. Regardless of this fact, God calls Common Law Unions fornication! That sounds worse than the world puts it doesn't it? Believers ought to realize that we cannot take our cues from the world; it's just not possible if spiritual growth is going the take place. There's a Jamaican saying "*Yuh can't buy a puss in a bag*" which means that it's foolhardy to purchase something you have not seen. Ironically that's how faith works – your decision to act is based on a trust. That's why I believe it is so important to be severely honest with each other when your relationship gets to the point that you are discussing marriage and put God at the center of your decision making plans.

10. I sense the restlessness in the person I have been dating for a few years now.

What do I do if I do not feel it is time to get married?

It's never wise to rush into marriage especially out of a sense of 'duty'. Marriage is a decision that both parties are to make together. One is not to force the idea on the other. A decision for marriage means a decision to take your relationship for the long haul. You would hate yourself (and perhaps your husband/wife too) if you disregard this feeling of indecision and it later rears its head as a point of discord when disagreements in your marriage arise (as they will if you both live long enough), and *"That's why I never wanted to..."* becomes a part of the tune you sing.

Jointly reassess your relationship to see if your long term goals regarding the progress of the relationship are the same as the person you are dating. That will help you determine if marriage is indeed the next appropriate step for *both* of you.

If you are a believer then fasting along with prayer clarifies things much better than any other approach would.

11. **What if the church I attend doesn't seem to have *suitable* potential mates? Is it ok to 'church hop' in order to search for one?**

In many cases your intention can either make or break you. There is absolutely nothing wrong with 'putting yourself out there'. I referred to Ruth in Chapter Eight (you must read the book of Ruth in the Bible), and highlighted her attitude as she faithfully served. In Chapter Three of Ruth, her mother-in-law, Naomi, advised her to beautify herself and present herself to Boaz. Based on the Jewish cultural practice, that family needed to be redeemed by the nearest male relative since Ruth's husband, Mahlon, had died (it would be good to get a brief overview of this Jewish tradition as well). The focal point is however that Ruth did not just sit around waiting, she presented herself. Such actions however were on the heels of her acts of service. Her sole purpose in life was not to go in search of a husband; and it was her willingness to focus on acts of service that initially won her Boaz's attention and favor.

Before deciding to attend another church in the hope of finding a suitable mate, it is important that you do not lose sight of your major purpose, service to God. Secondly, ensure that the churches you decide to check out are Biblically sound, and that the dates you may find there mirror your passion for growth in faith. Losing sight of the first will make the second void.

Attending a specific church is important for accountability since developing friendships will mean you have someone to look out for you, help you pray and address other spiritual and physical needs in a more specific way than if you were a visitor. Therefore I am not advocating a refusal to become a part of a fellowship, but I am suggesting that if you believe your needs are not being met, then going where they may be, is not sinful. Although Scripture advises us not to forsake gathering[77], it doesn't say anything about sticking to one place for worship. If the churches you select are truly reflecting the God of the Bible, then go for it!

12. My friends have always said I am not married because I am too picky, and until I hit age thirty I thought they were wrong, now I wonder, are they right?

If by "picky" you mean you are a female hoping to marry a man with the wealth and wisdom of Solomon as well as the selflessness of the Apostle Paul; the

[77] Hebrews 10:25

physical dominance of Samson as well as the meekness of Joseph; the peacefulness of Ghandi yet the aggressiveness of General Maximus Decimus Meridius (Russell Crowe's character in Universal/DreamWork's 2000 *Gladiator*), then your friends may be on to something. Or maybe you are that male looking for the woman with the supermodel figure, but will chow down three slices of pizza instead of a stalk of celery, who's as bold as Amelia Earheart yet needy as that damsel in distress. With this kind of thinking you also may face a few obstacles.

All those characteristics cannot be found in one person. Recognizing this fact is not the same as settling, but is actually a sign of mature practicality. The Christian has one non-negotiable criterion – the prospective spouse must also be a believer in Jesus Christ. Everything else will be based on personality and life objectives. Naturally we can be flexible with these to some extent, but we must be careful not to ignore our standards only to avoid singleness as such an action will undoubtedly bring frustration later on in the relationship. I don't think we give God enough credit. He knows you and your desires, if you give Him more game time he's going to score, believe me you will get the desires of your heart[78]. There's absolutely nothing wrong with having standards and you should hold on to them as you simultaneously allow God's Spirit to lead you in your decision making. Unfortunately, the persons who often have the most "advice" early out, are noticeably absent when difficulties arrive. Do not allow the criticisms/ jokes of others to become the determining factor in your decision for marriage.

13. *The people at my church frown at the fact that I'm a mature single who dates several different persons. How should I respond to that?*

---

[78] Proverbs 37:4-5

The attitude perhaps stems from a misunderstanding about what dating is. Ideally, the initial dating period should be that time when you do ‘a discovery’, and this may be achieved through interaction with several different men/women. However, you are perhaps being viewed as a person ‘playing the field’ since society generally likes to attach some permanence to a couple’s relationship once they have been seen together in public.

It is important for your testimony that your intentions are not misrepresented or misunderstood. If your objective is to indeed seek someone with whom you are most compatible, before attaching a label to your relationship, you have to be careful not to give the impression that your romantic relationships are kin to a revolving door. Until you have zeroed in on a specific person, avoid giving the impression that your friendship goes beyond a casual relationship. Be careful to avoid gestures that may give the impression of a closeness that does not exist between you and the current date.

The persons you date also need to be very clear about what your intentions are lest they too be misled.

14. Can a person not desire marriage yet not desire 'complete' singleness?

Complete singleness certainly cannot refer to solitude or the believer could not be effective in reaching the "*uttermost part of the earth*"[79] with Christ's message of salvation. 'Compete singleness' must then refer to a decision to abstain from relationships that mimic those of a romantic nature outside of the bounds of marriage. I believe the secular world has duped us into believing there is a middle ground of some sort. It suggests that not everyone will desire the formal institution of marriage but can have all that is associated with it, and gives live-in or visiting relationships as the viable options.

---

[79] Acts 1:8

These lack the permanence of marriage and are considered as suitable if the individuals are not certain if they want to be committed to one person for the long haul. Interestingly however, such relationships do have a sexual component to them and according to the Word of God believers should not participate in these. Because of the seeming prevalence of such arrangements however, many persons, Christians included, have begun to be less skeptical of these unions though we recognize their direct violation of Biblical commandments.

From a Christian point of view the options are quite simple; either you will serve God as a single person or a married one. The crux of this matter is your genuine service to God. If a believer does not desire to be married, he/she must then be desirous of remaining single; and the relationships that this individual forms should not develop into romantic intimacy since, based on our natural, God-given makeup, our bodies will begin to crave that physical connection which should not be satisfied while we are unmarried.

Recognizing that complete sexual abstinence was a gift from the Lord[80], the Apostle Paul admonished that those who have not been so gifted were to indeed marry and satisfy that natural sexual desire[81]. The point is there is no middle ground when it relates to sexual relationships, for if a believer is desirous of having this he/she must then be married.

15. What is God teaching me if I just seem to be unlucky in love?

Scripture teaches that the life yielded to God is not based on luck, and even the negative experiences are deliberately allowed by Him[82] to achieve a greater divine objective[83]. This is why I would never agree with an idea that someone has

---

[80] 1 Corinthians 7:7

[81] 1 Corinthians 7:9

[82] Job 1

[83] John 9:3

been ‘unlucky’ in love. I would suggest however, that sometimes painful relationships may come from that *‘big picture’* of God’s that often is unclear to us; as well as they may be a result of poor decisions that we have made.

If there are lessons to be learnt, I propose that those experiences are teaching individuals to rush less and pray for God’s direction more; focus on what God would want to do through us more, and less on the gratification we immediately seek; recognize that God does not seek our harm or misery, but allows bad experiences to happen to make us stronger, show His power, and gain the ultimate glory[84]. This is not an attempt to gloss over the undeniably painful experiences that countless persons have had over the years. In fact, understanding that such experiences have a greater purpose will allow us to view our difficulties in a different light. The life of a Christian is rife with paradoxes: we live in the world but are not to be of it, we

[84] James 1; 2-3

should appreciate the daily gift of life but ought to recognize the eternality of our existence, God promises us earthly blessings but wants us to be joyful when we have less than favorable experiences. An awareness and acceptance of this expectation of life will make life more worthwhile and easier to live. Your life (as a believer) is not about luck, it's about living in God's plan.

SUGGESTED READING

The following is a list of books I have found very inspirational in my own walk with God and may be directly and indirectly related to some of the positions I have taken with regard to my approach on the issues of singleness and marriage. They therefore should prove to be useful reading material for you. Certainly I encourage that you also peruse other works by these authors.

Chapman, Gary. *Things I Wish I'd Known Before We got Married.* North field 2010

George, Elizabeth. *A Woman After God's Own Heart.* Harvest House Publishers 1997

Hammond, Michelle McKinney. *Ending the Search for Mr. Right*. Harvest House Publishers 2005

Sassy, Single, & Satisfied. Harvest House Publishers 2010

Pinnock, Winston. *The Death of the Unequally Yoked.* WGP Publishing 2000

Shook, Kerry and Chris. *Love at Last Sight.* Waterbrook Press 2010

Stanley, Andy. *The Principle of the Path: How to Get From Where You Are to Where You Want to Be.* Thomas Nelson 2009

Warren, Rick. *The Purpose Driven Life*, Zondervan 2002

APPENDIX A:

What others think (Questionnaire)

Attached is a questionnaire distributed to a few of my Facebook friends over the age of twenty. Of the 93 persons receiving questionnaires, 17 persons responded and here are the questions and the related results. The findings of this mini research are mainly supplementary to the information presented in this book. I thought it necessary to add the thoughts of those in my sphere to see how closely, if at all, they match with some of the more generally perceived notions of marriage.

Questionnaire

Purpose:

1. To get a cross section of individuals' view on marriage
2. To compile said information as data to be added to my research on the views of marriage

   No individual's name will be publicized, although based on my chosen medium (email) I will know who different viewpoints belong to. There are no wrong or right answers the data is purely intended to get your take on the issue.

1. Are you a born again believer in Jesus Christ? Yes / No
2. Are your **M**arried *(skip questions 5-7)* / **S**ingle *(go to questions 5, 6, 8-11)* / **D**ivorced / **S**eparated *(go to questions 7-11)*?
3. How did you know he/she was *the one*?
   a. God, through prayer, revealed it to you
   b. It was a risk you decided to take

c. The situation compelled you
d. It was *time* since you'd been dating for a while
e. Your mutual love
f. Other (please explain)

4. Knowing what you do now would you make the same decision concerning marriage Yes / No

5. Do you want to be married Yes / No (skip question 6)

6. Why do you want to be married? (select all that apply)
    a. Sex
    b. Companionship
    c. Love
    d. God's work
    e. Status / respect
    f. Financial relief
    g. Age
    h. Desire for children
    i. Other (please explain)

7. Why did you get separated / divorced?
    a. Infidelity
    b. Grew out of love

c. Different goals materialized
d. Abuse
e. Other (please explain)

8. Do you think society suggests that marriage makes people
   a. Happier Yes / No
      Your view Yes / No
   b. More respected Yes / No
      Your view Yes / No
   c. Less lonely Yes / No
      Your view Yes / No

9. Do you find it odd when persons express a desire to remain single? Yes / No (skip question 10)

10. You think such a desire is
    a. Unnatural
    b. Selfish
    c. Impossible for sexual purity
    d. Dumb
    e. Other (please explain)

11. Other related comments you might want to add.

APPENDIX B:

Here's What They Think (Results)

Of the respondents, 88% percent professed to have a personal relationship with Christ, 47% is single, 35% married, and 18% is divorced/ separated.

Of the married, 24% admitted to having made their decision based on the answer they received from God through prayer, while 67% based their decision on the mutual love felt between their spouses and themselves. 50% however believe they would make a different decision concerning marriage had they been armed with the knowledge they now have.

100% of single respondents desired to be married. The most common reasons being a desire for sex and companionship, which featured in 75% and 100% of the answers respectively. 38% included a desire to procreate as part of their reason for desiring marriage, while 38% saw the role of God's work as an additional factor, and 25% sighted love as one of the reasons behind their desire for marriage.

Most interesting of the answers hinged on the impressions persons have of marriage:

65% of the respondents agreed that they believe society views married persons as happier than unmarried persons yet only 35% admitted to that being actually true. 76% believe that society conceptualizes that being married garners more respect for individuals yet only 29% actually believe that being married accords those individuals greater respect. Though 88% believe that society sees marriage reducing loneliness, only 35% believe that this is really true.

Of the 29% that found it odd for a person not to desire marriage: 40% thought the desire to be unnatural while 20% each saw it as a mark of selfishness or thought that there would be an inability for sexual purity to exist if someone opted to remain single. The remaining 20% expressed resulting loneliness or an incompleteness stemming from singleness.

The final question permitted respondents to share personal views related to the topic. I have included all the responses of those who opted to share them.

"I support marriage for everything that it has to offer"

"Marriage isn't for everyone and I don't think that someone should be forced into marriage or coerced because that is the 'norm'."

"I view marriage as such a huge commitment that carries enormous responsibility. I therefore ascribe a level of maturity to persons who have taken that path and seek to do it well."

"There is little acceptance in churches today of marriages that are struggling. Keeping it real and acknowledging real issues without judgment and condemnation, not in our experience!"

"I want marriage because I don't want to live my life alone or be caught up in boyfriend, baby mama and '*I thought he was single but is a married man*' drama. I want my own!"

"Marriage is a lot of work, it takes dedication, patience, compromise, constant effective communication and if persons cannot do any of those, then marriage is not for that individual. Couples have to constantly take the time to work on solving any little problem that comes up to live a happy life together."

"A desire to remain unmarried shows great satisfaction with God's purpose and your character; but above all it shows the proclamation of one of God's greatest gifts to us -the power of choice."

"I would stay married to my husband although he committed adultery... I don't like the idea of a divorce."

"I would prefer a culture that allowed many wives in my next life."

"I think the church has a lot to do with the decision people make about marriage. I think some denominations such as the Pentecostal and the Adventist church encourage people to get married quite young to 'save' them from sexual sin, as if that is the only reason to get married. I also don't think that enough is being preached to that section of the congregation who wants to remain single."

www.ingramcontent.com/pod-product-compliance
Ingram Content Group UK Ltd.
Pitfield, Milton Keynes, MK11 3LW, UK
UKHW021653190726
13853UKWH00001B/226

9 789768 230508